We were Number One, it seemed like yesterday,
Billboard said "These boys are on their way."
Very first song we sang sold a million strong;
now we can't figure out what the hell went wrong.

We lost our girls when the song hit ten,
we sit around broke remembering when
life was easy, so much fun:
it's a long way down... from Number One.

--the Highwaymen *In Concert* (2002)
"Number #1" (D. Fisher/A.B. Clyde)

Dedicated
to the memory
of
Chan Daniels

AUTHOR'S NOTE

When I was a little bitty baby
my Mama used to rock me in the cradle,
in them old cotton fields back home…

--the Highwaymen *Standing Room Only* (1961)
"Cotton Fields" (H. Ledbetter)

The "Great Folk Music Scare"—a term attributed to both Dave Van Ronk and Martin Mull-- was but a brief blip on the radar screen of modern popular music: just a few short years in the late 50s and early 1960s, at the peak of the Folk Revival, when the resurgence of the folk song seemed to threaten the dominance of rock n' roll. But in that brief span so much was achieved, thus there is so much to tell. And a great many people contributed to the making of this very personal but hopefully comprehensive account of both the Folk Revival and "Great Folk Music Scare"—their roots, highlights, and aftermath—through the story of the original Highwaymen.

First off, very special thanks to those surviving members of the original Highwaymen who spoke with me, emailed me, wrote to me, sent me stuff, and otherwise demonstrated extreme patience with my well-meant intrusions. Bob Burnett, Steve Butts, Dave Fisher, and Steve Trott have put up with a lot from me. I hope they find the end result at least somewhat satisfying compensation. Conversations and, in some cases, correspondence with many others, including Oscar Brand (I could listen to his stories for hours), Johann Helton, Ken

i

Greengrass, and Moses Henry McNaughten also helped. I am most grateful to all.

Deepest appreciation to any and everyone who took the time to go over the manuscript for errors of any kind, including the four original Highwaymen and their long-time personal manager—all of whom checked my facts—along with friends who read the book at my behest, like Janice Noble, Peter Forbush, the late John B. Pierce, Lisa Jayne Gordon, Rich Gamble, Suzanne Levasseur, Cary Mansfield, Norah Dooley, Rob Ayres, and Craig Lister. The encouragement of my colleagues and support from the folks at the Fraternal Order of Eagles have also helped to fuel my historical passion and productivity. I want to especially thank Lee Williams, who put up once again with my dangling participles and split infinitives as she corrected my writing for the more mundane but no less significant errors of grammar, spelling, and punctuation. Any remaining mistakes are solely my responsibility.

Likewise any problems with the four Appendices are entirely my fault. Appendix A relates exclusively to the Highwaymen and is compiled from Steve Koljanian's terrific discography work, as well as my own researches (and the stuff on the most recent CDs is completely my own). Appendices B and C overlap the Highwaymen with other folk artists, especially groups who experienced commercial and chart success from 1950 on, and any opinions or evaluations expressed are entirely mine. The information was derived mostly (although not exclusively) from online sources, as was the list of World Folk Music Association Awards in Appendix D. While this section has nothing to do with the Highwaymen specifically, I feel that it is important to acknowledge the tremendous work Dick Cerri and the WFMA have done to promote "contemporary and traditional folk music, spreading the word to fans, and keeping the folk community informed and involved."

Online research also came up with Bruce Eder's excellent article from allmusic.com, although it contains a few misconceptions and omissions which I hope this work takes care of. The lengthy liner notes (by Dave Fisher and Steve Koljanian) from the CD *Michael Row The Boat Ashore: the best of the Highwaymen* (EMI 1992) were also a terrific source of information. Steve Butts' guest stint on Wisconsin Public Radio's *University of the Air* in 2002 was extremely enlightening, as were the more personal, descriptive passages in Bob Dylan's memoirs. In addition, two books which came to my attention after I had completed the initial manuscript of *"NUMBER #1"*—Dave Van Ronk's *The Mayor of MacDougall Street* and Dick Weissman's *Which Side Are You On?*— assisted in reinforcing some of the broader, more sweeping assertions herein. They are delightful and highly informative books, both providing very personal perspectives on the era, while the latter demonstrates a genuine scholarship and depth that only someone as accomplished as Mr. Weismann can evoke. Any errors, differences of opinion, omissions, and idiocies are entirely my own.

Regularly researching online, closely reading the texts found on several albums and CDs, delving busily through books and articles amassed over time, and carefully utilizing data garnered from dozens of collectibles (many of them from ebay) provided a rich treasure trove of helpful material. Likewise, original correspondence pertaining to the group's initial foray into the professional world, made available by Steve Trott, added a great deal of insight into that period. This is not a formal work of academic scholarship. There are no elaborate footnotes or detailed citations. Sources are recognized here and at the end of this work, while other people's words and ideas are attributed within the text or by quotation. It is as much a story told through analysis and opinion as it is a history: something of a personal piece, as many of the events I describe began at about the same time I did.

You see, I was born during the same autumn that five young men were arriving as freshmen on the campus of Wesleyan University in Middletown, Connecticut. Bob Burnett, Steve Butts, Chan Daniels, David Fisher, and Steve Trott came from various places and each brought with him a variety of experiences, yet they all had in common a love of music, both playing and singing. It was this shared passion that would bring them together and grow into the folk music phenomenon that was the original Highwaymen. Their timing couldn't have been more fortunate, as the Kingston Trio and folk music were just hitting it big at the crest of the Folk Revival, emerging as apparently successful competition for the rock n' roll and pop music crowd—hence "The Great Folk Music Scare".

I had an uncle who was at Wesleyan in the late 50s and early 60s with the Highwaymen (a few years older than they, he actually graduated with them after a stint in the Marine Corps), and he brought home with him a couple of their earliest albums. My brother, ten years my senior, enjoyed the Highwaymen records and bought three of their later LP releases. So my sister and I grew up listening to the music of the Highwaymen, and their folk-themed harmonies were an important part of our musical upbringing.

The first five Highwaymen albums were constant companions throughout my childhood and early teen years. When I was sixteen, Ann Mayo Muir joined Gordon Bok on the stage of Benson Auditorium at St. Mark's School in Southborough, Massachusetts for a folk concert. After the show, I had a chance, albeit briefly, to talk with her about her experience with the group on the live LP *Hootenanny with the Highwaymen*. A little over a year after that encounter, I enrolled at Trinity College in Hartford, Connecticut, where Wesleyan University—home to the genesis of the Highwaymen—was our great athletic rival. I became a member of a pop-folk group on campus, the Trinity Pipes, who were not all that unlike the Highwaymen, although we were co-ed. Our repertoire covered lots of folk songs: we performed our rendition of the Highwaymen's "Marching to Pretoria", and we had an arrangement of "Well, Well, Well". We also sang "Julianne" from the New Christy Minstrels, "If I Had My Way", "City of New Orleans", and other folk tunes. I even learned to play the upright bass (shades of the Brothers Four and the Limeliters), although never very well. During that time, my sister sent me a couple of cassettes on which she had recorded those five cherished Highwaymen albums. I practically wore them out, playing them in my car while driving all through New England. As a counselor at and later Director of a summer camp for inner city kids, I encountered more Highwaymen tunes while singing around the evening campfire—"Michael" and "Big Rock Candy Mountain" were both favorites at Brantwood Camp. "Take This Hammer" and "Cotton Fields" were also sung there, along with other folk songs, like "Rattlin' Bog" (revived by Schooner Fare in the 70s and 80s), and especially the Weavers' "On Top of Old Smoky". I went on to teach, marry, and start a family. Still, those Highwaymen tapes stayed in the glove compartment of every car I owned. Even as I was getting on with my life, the Highwaymen remained a part of it.

It was in 1992, with the release of the greatest hits CD *Michael, Row the Boat Ashore: the best of the Highwaymen*, that my active interest in the group was revived. The detailed liner notes that

v

accompanied that collection told of an additional five albums of which I had been unaware. A handful of songs from those albums were featured on the CD, which only served to pique my curiosity. After another decade of collecting Highwaymen records and Highwaymen memorabilia, I finally got to meet the group at their 40th Anniversary concert on the Wesleyan campus: thus the genesis of this work.

But this is much more than the story of a single folk group in the early 1960s. From 1950 through the mid-60s there was a popular folk music revival here in the United States and throughout much of the world. "The Great Folk Music Scare" (essentially 1959-1964) took by surprise both concert promoters and record producers. Lasting barely six years—a short window of opportunity for a popular music genre (even disco lasted almost a decade)—its impact was felt not so much by its position on the charts as by its influence on what would follow. At the same time, it was a natural continuation of a rich folk music tradition, part of a series of folk revivals which in themselves were the inheritors of a folk music legacy going back decades, even centuries.

This story of the original Highwaymen then also serves as a lens through which can be viewed the last folk music revival of the twentieth century. They did not begin it—that distinction belongs to the Weavers and their powerful influence on the music scene. Nor did they trigger the "Great Scare"—that honor goes to the Kingston Trio with their dazzling commercial popularity. But the Highwaymen were an important part of all of it. Not only that, but they experienced the kind of popular chart achievement surpassed only by the aforementioned Trio and the subsequent Peter, Paul, & Mary (the era's culminating folk success story), while existing as a bridge between these two phenomena. Like the Kingston Trio and the Brothers Four, the Highwaymen emerged from the collegiate folk scene. Unlike those two groups but like PP&M, the Highwaymen were east coast, not west coast, folkies, and New York's Greenwich Village—vital to any account of this period—played a significant role in their adventures. The Highwaymen sang traditional folk songs in several different languages but with an emphasis on commercial performance. They therefore straddled the great divide that had always conflicted folk music, while representing the variety of strands which found expression in the work of a wide range of other folk artists. Finally, like many after the door closed on that era, they went their separate ways.

Yet they remain true to their roots, and they have survived. Of the other folk groups that flourished during the early sixties and are still performing and recording regularly today, only two or three retain a singing lineup of all original members—Peter, Paul, and Mary, sometimes the Chad Mitchell Trio, and… the Highwaymen. Through them, I hope to trace folk music history, particularly its popular (some might say "commercial") manifestations, from its earlier days through to those artists who were influenced by, as well as evolved from, folk music tradition. Still, while this is far more than simply a cut-and-paste compendium of folk music history, this is **not** the definitive history of folk music. It is simply the telling of a story through which one might discern **a** history of folk music, particularly the legacy of those folk groups which emerged during the fifties and early sixties, with the Highwaymen narrative as a road map for the journey. My sincerest apologies if readers feel I have left something or someone out. I have tried to provide this work with as much detail as possible, but a comprehensive overview of popular folk music history was never my goal. Whether appearing in these pages or not, all folk artists should feel represented here, if only by the spirit of folk music which is eternal and all-encompassing: hence Appendices B and C. I do expect that most of those who pick up this tome will already have some investment in the subject. Certain assumptions are made, such as an awareness on the reader's part of the differences (and similarities) between an LP and a CD, as well as the distinctions between a 78 record, a 33 record, a 45 record, a 7" disc, a reel-to-reel tape, a cassette, and even an 8-track. There will be no glossary provided, so the word "album" can (and does) mean almost anything within these pages. Be brave and read on!

Particularly challenging, of course, is to write about music using only words. When describing a melody or a song, words simply aren't enough. It would be great (and highly impractical) to include a comprehensive CD with this work, and even that would leave much out (as I am sure these pages do). It is my hope that reading this narrative might bring to each reader's mind and ear the memories of music past, and that fondly-recalled tunes and harmonies will fill their heads. Perhaps this work might even inspire some to go out and find the recordings all these talented artists have made—and in many cases are still making—and get to know them directly, through their music, rather than indirectly, through the written word. One lives in hope!

Again, a heartfelt "thank-you!" to all those mentioned before, especially to the Highwaymen themselves. And particular thanks to those other, more lasting Highwaymen fans—Elaine Haagen, Cathy Burnett, and Carol Trott—who are ever so gracious and welcoming to this wandering Highwaymen enthusiast. I will always be grateful for their kind acceptance.

The influence of J. Stanley Sheppard on my musical evolution, as well as his impact on my appreciation for music history, was indeed profound. Thank you, Stan!

The folks at Outskirts Press—particularly the oh-so-patient Michelle C. — have also been extremely helpful in the development of this book and the realization of its publication. To them I am sincerely indebted.

It is my family, however, to whom I owe my greatest debt. Thanks are due to my uncle Tim, who first introduced me to the Highwaymen, as well as to my brother Jared and my sister Maggie, who along with me enjoyed their music during those early years. Janice, my lovely and loving wife, deserves much praise and appreciation for her patience with my folk music obsession. Without her support, none of this would be possible. Likewise, I am grateful to my daughter, Martha, for her encouragement, and to my son, Jonathan, who has endured this music with (mostly) patient forbearance during our long drives. I know he wouldn't admit it, but even he likes some of it. Not bad for a twenty-first century teenager.

So the Highwaymen continue to sing, here at the dawn of the 21st century, some four decades after the last folk music revival of the twentieth. Their music, like all folk music, is forever.

Richard E. "Nick" Noble
Worcester, Massachussetts
October 2008

PRELUDE

Looking Back

We sang Michael Row the Boat across the land
when nobody'd ever heard of a rock n' roll band.
We loved the girls and just adored their screams,
and our heads were filled with dollar signs and dreams.

--the Highwaymen *In Concert* (2002)
"Number #1" (D. Fisher/A.B. Clyde)

Success took them by surprise. Months before, the five boys had given up on any serious dreams of music stardom. Their sole LP, recorded almost a year earlier, had been released in January of 1961, with their one and only single. The lack of popular response had been deafening, and United Artists, who had signed them to a contract with such high expectations, quickly dropped them from the label. It had been a disappointment, surely, but while they still harbored hopes, they also had other interests and greater ambitions. As their junior year wound down they made vacation plans, none of which included the singing summer job they had gone in search of two years previously. Bob Burnett, Steve Butts, Chan Daniels, Dave Fisher, and Steve Trott would begin their summer vacation in June, with almost three months ahead of them until reuniting at Wesleyan as seniors in the fall. With much to look forward to, and despite their remaining individually and occasionally optimistic, they were fairly certain that their salad days as the Highwaymen were behind them.

But then something unusual began to happen. Urged on by individual record promoters and DJs, the B-side of their single, "Michael", began to slowly climb the charts. Bob Burnett, far off in Nigeria, knew none of this. Chan Daniels, only a little bit closer, at his home in Argentina, was probably also unaware. Even Steve Trott and Dave Fisher, while in the States for much of that summer, caught on only gradually. Steve Butts, in New York and working as a broadcast engineer for WRVR-FM there, was perhaps the first to realize what was really happening. In mid-summer, "Michael" entered Billboard's Hot 100. Just a few days after Butts had finished working a twelve-hour folk concert broadcast featuring many of the great folk performers of the time, the song reached #1 in Toronto and broke into the U.S. Top 40. As the various members of the Highwaymen began to prepare for their return to campus in September, it was clear that a startling phenomenon was underway. On September 4, "Michael" topped the U.S. charts and remained there for almost a month. During their first days back at Wesleyan, the five seniors were now national celebrities.

While several folk and folk-type songs had charted since the 1940s, number one songs had been rare for real folk music in the twentieth century. The Weavers' "Goodnight, Irene" held the top spot for thirteen weeks in 1950, and interest in folk music had been reignited by the Kingston Trio's "Tom Dooley", which reached number one in mid-November of 1958. Since then, however, despite folk music's overall rise in popularity, thirty-four months and fifty-two number-one singles went by without a single genuine folk song reaching the top position. Then came "Michael" and the

Highwaymen. This was not necessarily a good thing, at least in the eyes of folk purists. The split between folk traditionalists and more commercial folk performers had always been there, but they had become even more sharply divided during the 1950s and into the early 60s. Old school folkies of that era were often considered radical and even dangerous by those in authority. In April of 1961, squads of New York City police were sent out to silence folksingers in Greenwich Village's Washington Square Park. Meanwhile, the major record labels and concert promoters were just beginning to figure out that folk music could sell commercially, but they found it unfamiliar territory. *"That's* folk music?" one perplexed executive exclaimed at the Highwaymen's first formal audition in late 1959.

Of course, the exact nature of folk music and a precise definition of the genre remain topics of much debate and controversy even within folk music circles; perhaps **especially** within folk music circles. As recently as 1995, Mark D. Moss, the editor of *Sing Out!* Magazine, wrote that "our community vehemently refuses to take responsibility for defining folk music." Moss himself took the inclusive view: folk music is a kind of umbrella, covering a variety of styles—blues, ballads, traditional, ethnic, and contemporary, among others. Folk scholar Samuel Forcucci agreed with Bruno Nettl and Helen Myers: "a broad definition of folk music is that it is music of the 'folk' or of the people." After that, however, things seem to get a bit more complicated.

Forcucci in 1984 listed eight criteria for an authentic folk song: that it should tell a story, that it should be the musical expression of common people, that it should have an unknown author (insisting that those songs with known authors were simply "patterned to fit the mold" of a 'typical' folk song"), that it should be colloquial, highly singable, simply structured, effective when unaccompanied, and indigenous to a particular region. Forcucci is generous enough to make a fair and balanced distinction between "traditional" folk songs and "modern urban folk" music. Others, however, have not been so flexible. An intransigent insistence on oral tradition, anonymous authorship, rural roots, and sometimes even genuine antiquity has highlighted the arguments of many folk purists. Refined performance is often seen as corrupting; commercial success viewed as a kind of sell-out.

It was musicologist Charles Seeger, certainly an appreciator of the classical folk music archetype, who argued that defining folk music should reject any "rigid boundaries" and should recognize many different types: primitive or tribal, elite or artistic, traditional folk, and popular. The Highwaymen can be said to have embraced all of these categories at one time or another. Even more significantly, they have expressed themselves in a repertoire that has included all four of the principal styles of folk song (whatever their type or origin): ballads—which tell stories; folk songs—being shorter, more lyrical and personal; spirituals—uniquely American, with roots in African tradition; and sea chanties, or shanties. This encompassing of varied types and styles, combined with their affinity for different languages, their cultivating of traditional folk roots (the majority of the cuts on their first three albums were older traditional folk songs), their later willingness to experiment with more recent folk compositions, and their emphasis on polished performance (not to mention their ultimate commercial success), put the Highwaymen directly in the middle of the last great folk revival, and thus an exemplar of that experience.

No one really saw it coming, however. It seemed to almost

everyone in the music business that rock n' roll was indeed "here to stay", with formal nods to the efforts of established solo performers like Frank Sinatra, and with plenty of room for Broadway tunes, Hollywood hits, and the occasional novelty act. Country music was the up-and-coming sound outside the mainstream. With its roots in folk but its heart in Nashville, the country sound seemed to have supplanted any kind of folk trend. The newly established Grammy Awards (they were first presented in 1958) had no category for folk music, but they had an award for Best Country & Western Performance. Yet beneath the surface, folk music was still there. Indeed, it had never left. "Folk music has been with us since the dawn of history," wrote Samuel Forcucci. And it is in that long, rich history, that the seeds of folk revival were sown.

I

1506-1958

River, take me along

in your sunshine sing me your song

ever moving and winding and free

you rolling old river

you changing old river

let's you and me river roll down to the sea.

--the Highwaymen *In Concert* (2002)

"River" (B. Staines)

Ancient cultures and tribal traditions were the beginning of folk music. It was carried over from year to year, decade to decade, century to century by word of mouth, through oral transmission. Only much later than its beginning would a song be written down, such as the "Song of Deborah" in the *Book of Judges*. During the first thousand years and more of the new millennium, wandering bards, minstrels, and balladeers journeyed around the world, traveling rivers and roads singing their songs and stories. Epic ballads, country melodies and intricate madrigals evolved side by side over time.

The earliest of these songs printed in English only appeared in the 16th century. These were Broadside Ballads, large single sheets featuring only the words—it was assumed the reader knew the familiar tunes. *A Lytle Geste of Robyne Hood* was published in 1506. In 1520, an Oxford bookseller recorded the sale of 190 Broadside Ballads, while from 1557-1709 the Stationer's Company of London collected 4p each in licensing fees for the printing of more than three thousand different ballads. From the late 16th century on, beginning with Richard Jones' *A Handfull of pleasante delites* in 1584, collections of ballads, known as Garlands, became available to the public. "Greensleeves", still a favorite, was featured in that first-ever folk songbook.

Folk music in the 18th century was both regional and topical. A number of what we would today call folk songs emerged from the American Colonial period and the War for Independence. On plantations throughout the American south, the first Negro spirituals could be heard as work songs, sung by black slaves to sustain them in their labors, many encoded with calls for freedom. Included among these was a chant intoned by slaves living among the islands off the coast of Georgia as they rowed back and forth between their quarters and the mainland, which a century-and-a-half later would become the Highwaymen's "Michael". Backbreaking work was also at the heart of developing sea chanties, or shanties, sung by sailors as they raised a sail or turned the capstan.

The 19th century saw the first commercialization of folk music. Stephen Foster wrote and composed songs inspired by both slave spirituals and rural country tunes. In Europe, Johannes Brahms worked with Hungarian folk melodies. Franz Schubert also experimented with folk songs to great success. But for old, traditional folk songs to impact the general public consciousness, history would have to wait for Francis James Child.

Born in 1825, the son of a sailmaker in Boston, Massachusetts, Child attended the Boston Latin School (the oldest public school continuously operating in the United States and the alma mater of Benjamin Franklin). Impressed with young Child's ability and potential, the Head Master of Boston Latin, Epes Sargent Dixwell, made a generous financial contribution to enable the boy to matriculate at Harvard. Francis James Child graduated in 1846, first in his class, and he was immediately offered a teaching position at the College. Over the next few years, young Child would teach mathematics, history, and political economy at Harvard, until in 1851 he was named the University's Boylston Professor of Rhetoric and Oratory. For a quarter century, while serving his alma mater in that position, Child collected hundreds of Broadsides and Garlands in many languages. After his retirement from the lecture hall in 1876, Child began working on his life's great achievement—five volumes entitled *The English & Scottish Popular Ballads*—which came out between 1882 and 1898. In creating this magnum opus, Child relied on his extensive collection, as well as on his correspondence with English experts in the field, such as Sabine Baring-Gould, the author of the hymn "Onward, Christian Soldiers", who had, throughout the 1880s, been collecting traditional folk music from Devon and Cornwall.

Child published more than three hundred ballads, many of them stark and grim, with others lushly romantic. His focus was on the words, their themes, and the history behind the story. Music was not an emphasis of Child's research. In an addendum at the end of the final volume, Child provided melodies, some only a single line or even just a fragment, for barely one-sixth of his published ballads. Still, Child Ballads have remained a staple on the set lists of countless folk singers throughout the 20th century and beyond. The Highwaymen would release recordings of two Child Ballads—#113, "The Great Silkie of Sule Skerrie" twice (in 1961 and again in 2003) and #217, "The Broom of the Cowdenknows" (in 2004).

In America during the post-Civil War period, the public was being made aware of the rich tradition of Negro Spirituals by the Jubilee Singers from Fisk University. Beginning in 1871 and continuing through the early years of the 20th century, the Jubilee Singers in various permutations toured the nation and the world. Although popular interest in African-American folk music waned after the start of the new century, it would not be long before its moving power would again revive and reemerge.

In 1889, the Folk Song Society was founded in England. Collectors of folk songs such as Lucy Broadwood, Kate Lee, and Frank Kidson established an organization that corresponded regularly with Americans like F.J. Child and fellow British enthusiasts like Baring-Gould. In the wake of this renewed commitment to folk music in the British Isles, there would emerge the first great 20th century authority on folk songs on both sides of the Atlantic, Cecil Sharp.

Cecil Sharp was just over forty at the turn of the century when he began his study of folk songs. Behind him was a London childhood, a decade spent living in Australia (where he founded the Adelaide College of Music), and a more recent post as a music teacher at a North London prep school. From 1904-1907 he would occupy the position of Music Tutor to the Royal Household, providing instruction on singing and playing to two future Kings of England. But from the moment he saw the Headington Quarry Morris Men give an exhibition of Morris Dancing to traditional country music,

Cecil Sharp was captivated by the folk genre.

In 1901, Sharp joined the twelve year-old Folk Song Society, but his serious pursuit of folk song collecting was still two years away. It was on August 22, 1903, that Sharp heard a Somerset country gardener going about his work and singing "The Seeds of Love". Delighted, Sharp wrote down both the words and the tune. He had begun his folk song "collection", and the century's first English folk song revival was underway. Over the next dozen years, he collected more than three thousand English folk songs, and from 1915-1918 some 1500 more during a series of visits to the Appalachian region of the United States. Sharp popularized folk music through lecture tours and by the publication of folk songbooks which sold quite well. Foreshadowing events and divisions a half-century in the future, the old guard of the folk music field considered Sharp to be something of an upstart; a "johnny-come-lately" besmirching the grand tradition of English folk songs with vulgar publicity and crass commercialism.

*　*　*　*　*　*　*　*

At Sharp's death in 1924, the first great folk revival was already on the wane, supplanted by the Jazz Age and the gentle pop crooning of such singers as Rudy Vallee. Still, folk music remained—to be heard around campfires, in union halls, on the Chautauqua circuit, and in the inner city. Homeless drifters would cook potatoes over a fire while singing "Big Rock Candy Mountain" (a traditional song, sometimes attributed to Harry "Haywire Mac" McClintock), while union meetings would echo with Joe Hill's "There Is Power In a Union" and "Workers of the World Awaken". Indeed, union activists would continue to rally around folk music over the next several decades. During the mine wars in West Virginia's Harlan County, Florence Reese, whose husband was one of the striking miners, took an old folk tune and adapted it into the now-classic standard of the labor movement "Which Side Are You On?". Individual folk artists also continued to perform during this era, tailoring the melodies to more classical styles of singing and playing. The 1920s saw the emergence of individual female performers in real numbers. Prominent among these was Ellinor Cook, who toured the country during the 20s and early 30s, singing folk songs of Europe and the world in their original languages (much as the Highwaymen were to do many years later), most often accompanied by pianist Camilla Leonard Edwards. With another accompanist, Eugena Folliard, Cook would also present a program of Polish folk songs to honor General Joseph Pilduski. Simultaneous with all of this, the Harlem Renaissance sparked renewed interest in African-American music, and arrangements of old spirituals and slave songs were popular with both black and white audiences. Paul Robeson's *Songs of Free Men* was a critically acclaimed recording of the time.

As folk singing continued to persevere, so did the legacy of Cecil Sharp, at least in the United States. Even as the Great Depression held America in its unforgiving grasp, pioneer folklorist John A. Lomax traveled through Appalachia and much of the rural south, recording folk songs using the then-newest technology. With Alan, his son, Lomax developed the Archive of American Folksong at the Library of Congress as a significant national resource. In 1933, Alan Lomax met Huddie Ledbetter, a convict serving a sentence for attempted murder at the Louisiana State Penitentiary. Ledbetter thrilled Lomax with his original songs, more than one hundred of which Lomax recorded over the next few days. Lomax then

6

produced a single record—"Goodnight Irene"—which so impressed Louisiana Governor Oscar "OK" Allen that he pardoned Huddie Ledbetter on August 1, 1934, and the legend of "Leadbelly" was born. In 1935, Lomax took Leadbelly on a tour of the north, where he became something of a sensation. It was a version of Leadbelly's "Cotton Fields" which would become the Highwaymen's second big hit, some thirty years later. With the advent of Alan Lomax's national radio show in 1939, Leadbelly was introduced to a national audience. The younger Lomax, by this time the Director of the Library of Congress' American Folksong Archive, also used his radio program to first present artists like Woody Guthrie, Burl Ives, and young Pete Seeger to the greater public. The century's second great folk revival had begun.

Woody Guthrie was from Oklahoma, and he traveled the nation from Texas to California during the depths of the Great Depression, writing and singing original folk songs. "Bound for Glory", "This Land is Your Land", "Going Down the Road"—a version of the latter recorded by the Highwaymen in 1962 under the title "Lonesome Road Blues"—are only a small part of his prolific musical legacy. By the end of the decade he had moved to New York City, but with the advent of the Second World War, he would be on the move again. Burl Ives had been an aspiring young actor on Broadway, but in his twenties he dropped out of college to travel the country as an itinerant singer, doing odd jobs and playing the banjo. In Mona, Utah, he was thrown in jail for singing "The Foggy, Foggy Dew", which local authorities considered bawdy and obscene. But he soon was out and resumed his peregrinations, sometimes performing in Depression-era encampments alongside Pete Seeger. The son of musicologist Charles Seeger, Pete Seeger often played at left-wing political functions in the 1930s with his friend Lee Hays. All of these performers appeared on Alan Lomax's radio show, as did other well-known folk artists of the period, such as John Jacob Niles and Cisco Houston—a close friend of both Woody Guthrie and Leadbelly. And in 1940, *Our Singing Country*, a book by John A. and Alan Lomax and Ruth Crawford Seeger (Pete Seeger's stepmother) was published to critical acclaim.

The advent of the 1940s saw Guthrie, Seeger, Hays, and Millard Lampell form the Almanac Singers, the first real folk group of the 20th century. They would be joined in their musical endeavors—performing and recording while based in a three-story rented house—by Bess Lomax, Sis Cunningham, Arthur Stern, Butch and Peter Hawes, Charley Polachek, Cisco Houston, and others. Left-wing radical in its politics, the group gave a memorable concert at the American Youth Congress in Washington, DC during February of 1941. The Almanac Singers produced two albums in their short time together. Their first—*Songs for John Doe*—advocated isolationism and was made with the support of Alan Lomax. The second—*Talking Union*—was even more radical and in many ways quite anti-Roosevelt. Guthrie's "The Union Maid" a classic take on an old traditional tune, came from this period.

Still, the Almanac Singers had their own individual pursuits as well. It was in May of 1941 that Woody Guthrie, on the recommendation of Alan Lomax, was hired by the U.S. Department of the Interior to write songs about the northwest—its people, its places, and the promise of low-cost power from the Bonneville Power Administration. In just thirty days, Guthrie composed twenty-six songs, including "Pastures of Plenty", "Hard Travellin'", and "Roll On, Columbia" (the latter would be recorded by the

Highwaymen more than two decades later, and would continue to be performed in their concerts well into the 21st century). After his one-month stint as a Federal employee, Guthrie would return to the more left-wing music of the Almanacs. Still, the invasion of the Soviet Union by Germany in July of 1941 saw a sudden change in the attitude of American radicals toward the European conflict. The tone of the Almanac Singers' recordings became decidingly anti-Fascist and pro-intervention, as exemplified by the Guthrie-Lampell-Seeger composition "Round and Round Hitler's Grave". One of the last songs from the Almanac Singers was "The Sinking of the Reuben James" by Woody Guthrie/Millard Lampell, which the Highwaymen would record twice, in 1964 and 2002. After Pearl Harbor, the Almanac Singers split up. Seeger and Hays would establish communal homes called Almanac Houses during the war years, while Woody Guthrie would once again take to the road, often with his friend Ramblin' Jack Elliott, sometimes with a young Canadian folksinger named Oscar Brand, busking (singing for their meals) as they traveled. On the side of Woody Guthrie's guitar was emblazoned the message: THIS MACHINE KILLS FASCISTS. Eventually, many of the Almanac Singers would enlist. Woody Guthrie served in the Merchant Marine, along with Pete Hawes and Cisco Houston. Brand would join the Army after his graduation from Brooklyn College in 1942. Pete Seeger and Lee Hays would also go into the armed forces, while Butch Hawes found employment as a welder for the war effort.

From 1940-1948, Burl Ives had his own radio show. Its title— *Wayfaring Stranger*—came from one of his hit songs. During the decade of the 1940s, Ives saw four more songs reach the charts. They were "The Foggy, Foggy Dew" (which no longer, it seems, led to his arrest), "Big Rock Candy Mountain" (which would also be recorded by the Highwaymen on their very first album), "Lavender's Blue (Dilly Dilly)", and his biggest hit—"The Blue-Tail Fly" which made it into the Top Ten.

In 1943, Woody Guthrie's autobiography, *Bound for Glory*, was published. In 1944, Guthrie and several of the Almanac Singers joined with the talents of Josh White, Tom Glazer, Burl Ives, Sonny Terry, and Brownie McGhee to record as The Union Boys for Moses Asch on New York's Asch Records. That same year, a new American folksinger, English-born Richard Dyer-Bennett, made his debut as a singer of Anglo-American songs, many of them Child Ballads. His trained voice and his scholarly, refined (some would say "European" or even "operatic") style helped make much of the folk repertoire palatable to a more classically-attuned audience. And folk music soon had another voice on the airwaves. Upon his discharge from the army in 1945, Oscar Brand became coordinator of folk music for New York's municipal station, WNYC, and he soon began the regular program *Folk Song Festival.* In contrast to these increasingly "respectable" forms of folk music, Pete Seeger helped establish "People's Songs" at his Greenwich Village house in 1946. A loose confederation of more radical songwriters and performers, "People's Songs" was intended to bolster postwar union and social activity, keeping alive the folk tradition of protest which had been founded in the socialist and union movements of the 1930s. Lee Hays, Cisco Houston, Frank Miller, and Richard Dehr were among those who joined Seeger in this New York endeavor. In the atmosphere of postwar anti-communism, witch hunts, and blacklists, their kind of folk music had gone underground. Seeger and Hays' old partner, Woody Guthrie, was also back in New York, and in 1947, his son Arlo was born there.

* * * * * * * *

Tragedy struck the folk world in 1949, when Huddie Ledbetter fell ill while on a European tour. Diagnosed with amyotrophic lateral sclerosis (Lou Gehrig's disease), he died on December 6, leaving behind a rich legacy of original music in the folk tradition. Leadbelly's work would not be forgotten. His creative brilliance would be celebrated through the efforts of a new folk group which had been formed that in same year, when Pete Seeger, Lee Hays, Fred Hellerman, and Ronnie Gilbert came together as the Weavers. A handful of unsuccessful recordings on the Charter Label had them thinking of disbanding after only a few months together. They decided to give it one last try, and they auditioned for and won a spot performing Christmas week at the Village Vanguard, a New York club. It was just a few weeks after Leadbelly's death, and the Weavers were a huge hit, their rendition of his "Goodnight, Irene" the highlight of the show. Held over for six triumphant months, they were approached by Gordon Jenkins and Decca records to cut an album of folk songs. To enhance their commercial appeal, the group would be supported by the big band sound of the Gordon Jenkins Orchestra, abetted by a background chorus on several numbers. In the summer of 1950, the Weavers took "Tzena, Tzena" all the way up to second place on the national charts, and they followed that success with Leadbelly's "Goodnight, Irene", number one for thirteen straight weeks, selling two million records. "On Top of Old Smokey" and "Wimoweh" (later performed by the Tarriers and eventually a pop hit as "The Lion Sleeps Tonight" by The Tokens) also charted for the Weavers that same year. Despite the fact that they were criticized by purists for their orchestrated sound and criticized by old leftist comrades as capitalist sellouts, the Weavers inspired and empowered the generation that would create "The Great Folk Music Scare" a decade later. Indeed, the Weavers were the bridge between the second great folk revival of the century, which they completed, and the millennium's last great Folk Revival, which they inspired.

The Highwaymen would record several Weavers songs, especially the works of Fred Hellerman ("I Never Will Marry" and "The Ladybug and the Centipede" among them). "Run Come See Jerusalem" was a Weavers song that the Highwaymen released on their third album. "Greenland Whale Fisheries", "I Know Where I'm Going", "Eres Alta", "Pretoria", "Sinner Man", and even "Michael" were among those songs found on earlier Weavers' albums which would be recorded and released by the Highwaymen. Eventually, the Highwaymen would record their version of "Goodnight, Irene" in the 1990s, honoring the Weavers as the great folk group of the early 1950s.

But it was all too good to last. Called before the House Un-American Activities Committee (HUAC) in 1951 to testify about his early communist connections, Pete Seeger refused to name names. The Weavers were blacklisted, and when they found they could no longer get air time or count on record sales, the group disbanded. There followed some tough years for Pete Seeger. In 1953 his stepmother, Ruth Crawford Seeger, renowned musicologist and folklorist, passed away. Seeger found intermittent work performing mostly at leftist events (such as a concert sponsored by the Cornell Labor Youth League on the campus of Cornell University). Activism was under fire during this time, and it was a less than inspiring period for folk music. Some performers, like the sincere and successful Richard Dyer-Bennett and the colorful and vibrant scholar and folklorist John Jacob Niles—with his special on-stage personality, his unique "dulcimo", and his repertoire of old Appalachian ballads—continued to get work. So did Burl Ives, who remained employable because he had cooperated with HUAC when he was called to testify. But even Ives' career was taking a different path—into acting and films, where he garnered critical acclaim in dramatic parts like Big Daddy in *Cat On A Hot Tin Roof.* In 1958 he would win an Academy Award for his supporting performance in *The Big Country.*

Folk music during this period was kept alive on both sides of the Atlantic in no small part through the efforts of two individuals. In Britain, Alan Lomax was spending some time as a field recorder and radio producer for the BBC. His endeavors there sparked a British folk revival, inspiring the likes of Lonnie Donnegan. This led to the musical style called "skiffle", which would ultimately be absorbed into rock n' roll and evolve into the Beatles, with the British invasion coming just a decade later. Back on this side of the water, Oscar Brand's long-running *Folk Song Festival* on New York Public Radio provided opportunities for performers like Pete Seeger (until the blacklist), Peggy Seeger, Dave Van Ronk, Ed McCurdy, and Brand himself, as well as for arrangements of Negro Spirituals by John N. Work and the Renaissance and Baroque offerings of The Deller Consort—Alfred Deller's Madrigal group, first founded in 1948. It was Brand who, at a New York concert to benefit miners' relief, introduced folksinger Jean Ritchie, one of the Kentucky Ritchies—the first family of Cumberland song—to the public. Amid a star-studded line-up featuring Pete Seeger, Burl Ives, and many more, Ritchie, recommended to Brand at the last-minute by Alan Lomax, was only supposed to perform one song. With her long red hair, her traditional dulcimer, and her wonderful voice, Ritchie captivated the audience for three-quarters of an hour, with Oscar Brand holding the microphone for her the entire time. Popular American folk music in the mid-1950s **was** Oscar Brand. And then the Weavers returned.

In 1955, after the fall of Senator Joseph McCarthy saw a lessening of public paranoia and a relaxing of political pressure, the Weavers gave a landmark reunion concert at Carnegie Hall. The live album of that concert on the upstart Vanguard label sold well, and the response from the traditional folk community was also warm. Gone were the orchestra and the backing chorus. This was a stripped-down, banjo and guitar group: the Weavers returning to their folk music roots. It failed to spark a commercial folk upsurge—competition from that new type of popular music, rock n' roll, saw to that—but it did mean that something very special would not be forgotten. The Weavers' return to the public eye in the late 1950s also coincided with the founding, by Israel Young in 1957, of the Folklore Center at 110 MacDougall Street in Greenwich Village. Obscure recordings, books and music, staged concerts, cider and cheese gatherings, and a mimeographed newsletter all combined to make Izzy Young's venture a mecca for folk aficionados, including Pete Seeger, Bob Dylan, and later the Highwaymen.

The Weavers continued even after Seeger left the group. He was replaced by Erik Darling, who had been part of the Tarriers, the first integrated folk group. The Tarriers (originally Darling, Bob Carey, and soon-to-be actor Alan Arkin) had a hit in 1956 with "The Banana Boat Song (Day-O)". That year, The Tarriers competed with Harry

14

Belafonte's recording of the same song which climbed into the top ten, giving that talented solo performer his greatest success. There were other fine folk groups during this period, including the Town Criers and the Gateway Singers—the latter featuring Lou Gottlieb and, for a short while, Travis Edmonson: their best song being "Midnight Special"—but most folk music in 1955, 1956, and 1957, at least in the popular perception, other than Oscar Brand's radio offerings, came from Harry Belafonte. His "Jamaica Farewell" was another Top 40 hit, rivaled in folk circles only by "Marianne" from Terry Gilkyson and the Easy Riders ("People's Songs" veterans Frank Miller and Richard Dehr), an enjoyable number with a Calypso flavor. Indeed, Harry Belafonte's two Calypso albums remained bestsellers for three straight years. Yet in 1957, two young men from Hawaii and a Stanford University graduate student would come together under a name inspired by Calypso's success, and they would forever change the face of popular folk music.

*　*　*　*　*　*　*　*

Bob Shane and Nick Reynolds had sung together at high school in Hawaii. By 1957 they were ready to leave California's Menlo College and pursue a career in music. In Palo Alto that year, they joined up with Dave Guard, who had been continuing his education at Stanford. Calling themselves the Kingston Trio, because the name reminded people of the then-popular Calypso music by Harry Belafonte, they began performing at college fraternity houses up and down the West Coast. In May of that year they won the job as comedienne Phyllis Diller's opening act at San Francisco's Purple Onion coffee house. Dave Guard guaranteed for the group a packed

15

hall and an enthusiastic reception by sending 500 postcards to their friends on the Stanford and Menlo campuses. Impressed with the group's success, the Purple Onion held them over after Diller's departure as headliners, and from June through December of 1957, the Kingston Trio topped the bill at San Francisco's trendiest nightspot.

Clubs like the Purple Onion would be the backbone of the folk revival that was just around the corner. It was while visiting San Francisco's folk clubs that the classically trained Odetta would first be exposed to and then turn her career toward folk music. Despite the central role played by New York's Greenwich Village in the folk movement over the next several years, "The Great Folk Music Scare" had its genesis in San Francisco, at the Purple Onion.

In the summer of 1957, the Kingston Trio signed a seven year contract with Capitol records. During this time they perfected their act, pacing themselves with comic banter and adding to their set list, until they had put together a real show almost two hours long. In December of 1957 the Kingston Trio started a national tour, playing such diverse venues as the Holiday Inn in Reno, Mr. Kelly's in Chicago, and the Village Vanguard in New York. The Trio recorded its first album in just three days, and their first single, "Tom Dooley" was released in July of 1958. Picked up by a DJ in Salt Lake City, "Tom Dooley" spent from October 1958 through January 1959 in Billboard's Top Ten, reaching number one, with ultimately more than three million in sales. At the 1959 Grammy Awards, the Kingston Trio emerged triumphant, but as there was no folk music category, they won for Best Country and Western Performance. As Bob Shane would later joke: they were the only country and western folk group from Hawaii with a Calypso name. Still, there was no doubt about it: television appearances and a second album which featured their live stage show saw the Kingston Trio firmly in place as the most successful and sought after group in America

Concert promoters were stunned. What would happen to the rock n' roll caravans and record label tours if what the public wanted was folk music? Record companies also took notice: maybe rock n' roll wasn't here to stay. "The Great Folk Music Scare" had promoters and producers scrambling for folk acts. Several would emerge over the next couple of years, among them a group of five young men from the campus of Wesleyan University in Middletown, Connecticut.

II

1958-1959

Once upon a time in the used-to-be
we were five of a kind, my friends and me...

--the Highwaymen *Still Rowing* (1999)

"The Glory Years" (D. Fisher/R. Davis/A.B.Clyde))

Wesleyan University was named for John Wesley, the founder of the Methodist movement which originated during the eighteenth century in England. Methodism, with its focus on personal faith, social responsibility, and education, had crossed the Atlantic by the early nineteenth century, and in 1831 Wesleyan University was founded in Connecticut at Middletown. There were just forty-eight students that first year, but the University grew rapidly over the subsequent decades. While the theological training of Methodist clergy was a primary emphasis at Wesleyan, from the very beginning it was also known for its curricular innovations. In 1937, Wesleyan University became fully independent from the Methodist Church, and following the Second World War, under the leadership of Victor L. Butterfield, the institution truly came into its own.

Butterfield, who had been elected President of the University in 1943, served in that position until 1967. During his twenty-four years at the helm, a number of new and exciting offerings were added to

19

the curriculum. Established in 1953, Wesleyan's Graduate Liberal Studies Program is the oldest Liberal Studies program in the country, and Wesleyan became the nation's very first University to offer a graduate degree in that area. Interdisciplinary study was strongly encouraged during Butterfield's tenure. Particularly significant was Wesleyan's innovative program in world music, or ethnomusicology, which was begun there in the mid-1950s. Professors such as David McAllester pioneered the study of musical traditions as part of anthropological research. By 1966, the Wesleyan University Press was able to publish *Ethnomusicology & Folk Music: An International Bibliography of Dissertations and Theses*, compiled by Frank Gillis and Alan P. Merriam. This, then, was the atmosphere that the Wesleyan Class of 1962 entered as freshmen in the fall of 1958.

That autumn, freshmen were rushed by the various fraternities on campus, including the Wesleyan chapter of Alpha Chi Rho (AXP). Wesleyan freshmen, including the incoming pledges to AXP, were soon challenged to provide some entertainment for the fraternity's upperclassmen and their dates. "We couldn't act," recalled Steve Butts, "and we couldn't do magic tricks, so we decided to sing." Butts was a native New Yorker and the son of the Dean of International Studies at Columbia University's Teachers College. He had been stricken with polio as a child and he walked with the aid of crutches. A square dance caller in high school, he also enjoyed singing, and his early college experiences would encourage him to keep up with the guitar and, later, learn the banjo. Butts had traveled much of the world, including some time residing in Australia, before coming to Wesleyan, and he intended to major in Government. While Stephen J. Butts certainly took his academic aspirations quite seriously, at that moment in October of 1958 the young eighteen year-old's chief concern was participating in a show.

Fellow freshman David Fisher, the son of a public school principal in New Haven, Connecticut, took the lead in organizing this endeavor. Already an accomplished musician, Fisher had experience on piano, guitar, banjo, and recorder. In high school he had played and sung with a successful rock n' roll doo-wop band called The Academics; his clear, high tenor impressive even then on upbeat numbers like "Something Cool", Fisher's very first songwriting effort. While he was still undecided about whether to major in psychology or music, Fisher had come to Wesleyan in part because of its musicology program, and he hoped someday perhaps to earn his PhD in that field. But all that was less important to him than exactly what kind of performance he and his new friends would put together. "I remember insisting we do primarily folk music," Fisher reminisced some thirty years later, "because 'college men' were expected to give up their childhood tastes." Still, top tenor Fisher and bass singer Butts joined Bob Burnett and Chan Daniels in quite a good imitation of Danny and the Juniors, singing "At the Hop" to an impressed gathering of local young ladies and their AXP escorts.

Burnett, the quartet's second tenor, came from Mystic, Connecticut, and was the son of a Boston investment broker. His father ran a cemetery, and young Bob's very first job was digging graves. Although slight of build, he was strong, wiry, and athletic. He enjoyed swimming, sailing, and singing. His involvement with his new friends inspired him to learn the guitar and take up both the bongo drums and maracas. An excellent athlete, Burnett would play hockey and run track at Wesleyan while majoring in Government there. Chan Daniels, who sang a strong baritone part, had been born and grown up in Buenos Aires, Argentina, where his father ran a large and successful American Motors dealership. Tall and well-mannered, he spoke fluent Spanish and had learned to play the guitar at an early age from his father. The elder Daniels' hobby was singing and collecting songs on tape. Chan Daniels had considerable singing experience during his high school years, and he also learned to play the charango, a ten-stringed South American instrument made from an armadillo shell. A diligent scholar, Daniels planned to major in History. At the show that evening, however, they set all thoughts of scholarly or athletic pursuits aside, and they sang both folk music and rock n' roll numbers, receiving a very positive response. "John Henry" was accompanied by Fisher on the piano. They also performed a couple of Irish and Scottish songs for the first time. And there was more rock n' roll. They enjoyed themselves immensely that evening. "We discovered that we liked singing together," said Butts. The next week they took their guitars to the lounge of the freshman dorm, where they started rehearsing, often providing a musical background to the less harmonious efforts of preoccupied pool players. They decided to jettison all their rock n' roll numbers. "We were looking, quite frankly, for better music," Steve Butts said. Their repertoire soon became exclusively "folksy", in Dave Fisher's phrase, inspired in no small part by the work of the Weavers.

Not long after the show, the four were joined at their rehearsals by a fifth freshman, Steve Trott. Originally from Glen Ridge, New Jersey, Trott had grown up in Mexico, where his father David was an executive in the overseas division of Procter and Gamble. While living south of the border, Trott learned to play guitar from a Mexican garbageman. Although he now made his home in Cincinnati, Trott had studied in Europe as well as Latin America, and he spoke both French and Spanish. He intended to major in Romance Languages at Wesleyan, but he also had his sights set on a law degree somewhere down the line. Trott had encountered Chan Daniels on his very first day at Wesleyan. Actually, they had met when they both had descended almost simultaneously from either end of the same railroad coach at the station in Meriden, Connecticut. Each noticed immediately that the other was carrying a guitar, and "like magnets," Trott would recall some four decades later, "our instruments drew us together." So Trott was interested in joining his friend, bringing with him his guitar and an affinity— shared by Daniels—for singing songs in languages besides English, particularly Spanish and French. Within months, they were performing at various spots around campus. They called themselves the Clansmen, because they had several Scottish and Irish tunes on their set list. They were, it seems, naively undisturbed by the name's homonymically negative connotation.

*　　*　　*　　*　　*　　*　　*　　*

Other than their name, Wesleyan's Clansmen were no different than many other folksingers emerging on the college scene. Like the Kingston Trio the year before, they were performing at fraternity houses and private parties on and around their own campus. Also in 1958, only a few hours drive north of Middletown, eighteen year-old Joan Baez was making her folksinging debut at Club Mt. Auburn 47, near Harvard in Cambridge, Massachusetts. A jazz joint which had turned itself into a folk venue on Tuesday and Friday nights, the club paid her ten dollars. Baez, from northern California and of Mexican, Scots, and Irish descent, performed "Black is the Color of my True

Love's Hair", a traditional melody. Soon she was appearing in coffee houses, small clubs, and other intimate venues around Cambridge and Boston. That same year, four University of Washington Phi Gamma Delta fraternity brothers had come together as The Brothers Four. Before long, Bob Flick, Mike Kirkland, John Paine, and Richard Foley were performing on campuses and at Seattle coffeehouses. Signed to a contract by Columbia records, their second single featured "Greenfields", a lush, brooding ballad by Terry Gilkyson, Frank Miller, and Richard Dehr. In late 1959, as the group successfully toured the country, the song began to climb the charts, eventually reaching the second spot in early 1960. That year, the Brothers Four were nominated for three Grammy Awards, and in 1961 their second hit, "The Green Leaves of Summer", would be nominated for an Oscar. The Brothers Four sound was smoother and more pop-music oriented than even the rough-edged but commercial Kingston Trio, yet both were essentially West Coast groups. Although California and Washington had their share of more traditional folk performers, most of these could be found on the other side of the continent, in New York City.

In 1958-1959, folk musicians like the classically trained gospel and spiritual singer Leon Bibb, Arkansas high school principal and collector of Ozark folk songs Jimmy Driftwood, Scottish-born Ewan MacColl, Irish singer and actor Tommy Makem, Canadian Alan Mills, and the versatile Ed McCurdy were performing in Greenwich Village. Theodore Bikel, a solo performer who, like the Highwaymen, would be known for singing folk songs from many cultures in their original languages, was also a Greenwich Village regular. A favorite venue was the Village Gaslight, later known as the Gaslight Café, at 116 MacDougall Street. Started by John

Mitchell, who had previously run the successful Figaro Coffee House on the corner of Bleecker and MacDougall, the Gaslight was literally excavated from beneath the main building above it. It was a cellar room, with dark brick walls and exposed pipes. The ceiling had been too low, so Mitchell, surreptitiously at night because he had no permit, simply shoveled out the dirt floor to the necessary depth, sneaking the excess earth out in sacks like an escapee from a World War II POW camp, dumping it in trash cans up and down MacDougall. Like the Figaro before it, the Gaslight was at first a basket house for Beat poets like Allen Ginsberg, Gregory Corso, and Hugh Romney (later and better known as Wavy Gravy). After each performer was done, a basket was passed, and if the audience liked what they heard, they dropped in some coins. Folk musicians were beginning to make themselves known at these basket houses, but there was considerable overlap. Ohioan Len Chandler tried his hand at reciting poetry at the Gaslight before emerging as a folk musician. Noel Paul Stookey, then a young comedian and singer, was an early master of ceremonies there. The police, always suspicious of the scruffy beatnik types who patronized these basket houses, were constantly trying to shut down the Gaslight on one pretext or another. When neighbors started to complain about the noise, the management would ask patrons to snap their fingers rather than applaud.

While the five young Clansmen at Wesleyan may have been oblivious to much of this, they were certainly not unaware of the Kingston Trio's terrific success. The Trio was atop the charts and playing two hundred dates a year. Steve Butts and the rest of the Clansmen went to see them in 1959 when they performed in Connecticut. All were impressed by their well-presented two-hour show, complete with comedic banter and formal arrangements of folk numbers old and new. The Kingston Trio dominated the popular music field, with as many as four top 40 albums on the charts at once by early 1960, including a live LP recorded at San Francisco's "hungry i". They were featured at the 1959 Newport Folk Festival (along with nineteen-year-old Joan Baez). On August 3, 1959, the Kingston Trio appeared on the cover of LIFE magazine. They were named Group of the Year by both Billboard and Cashbox, and they won two Grammy Awards.

And the Kingston Trio wasn't alone. They had already begotten at least one group, albeit indirectly. In 1959, Lou Gottlieb, a Doctor of Musicology and formerly of the Gateway Singers, had been hired by the Trio to scout out more folk material for them. In Hollywood, he encountered folksingers Alex Hassilev and Glenn Yarborough at the Cosmo Alley Nightclub. The three decided to form their own folk trio. That autumn, when they appeared at the hungry i in San Francisco, they were billed as the Limeliters, after the Limelite Lodge in Aspen, Colorado, where their group had made its debut.. The Limeliters became known for a unique sound, Gottlieb's effective arrangements, their delightful on-stage interaction, and a set-list of songs which (like the Highwaymen a bit later) included a variety of languages. More sophisticated and complex than their fellow West Coast groups, a famous quote from *Time* magazine explained their appeal: "If the button down scrubbed looking Kingston Trio are the undergraduates of big-time folk singing, The Limeliters are the faculty." While they were never blessed with tremendous hit singles, the Limeliters received a great deal of critical acclaim, their live shows were among the most erudite and entertaining on the folk circuit, and their albums always sold very well. Indeed, the Limeliters' LP "Through Children's Eyes", a double Grammy nominee, is still considered one of the finest albums for young people ever recorded.

*   *   *   *   *   *   *   *

Throughout all this, the Clansmen were singing "for hamburgers" according to Steve Trott, at campus venues and at more public events, such as local halls and dinner concerts all over Connecticut. The group was motivated by older, local Wesleyan folksingers, like the duo of Larry & Myra, from whom they first heard the Child Ballad "The Great Silkie", and the Clansmen began to expand their repertoire. They had their usual part-time jobs "like all college students," Trott recalled, "but we really loved playing the guitar and running around singing...

Our first couple of years at Wesleyan we'd show up anyplace—
fire in a toaster oven, cat in a tree—anywhere there was a crowd
we'd show up and sing a few folk songs. Then we decided 'Gee, this
is really fun; maybe we could get a summer job.'

III

1959-1960

On a summer's day in the month of May
a burly bum came hiking
down the shady lane through the sugar cane
he was looking for his liking.
As he strolled along he sang a song
of a land of milk and honey;
where a bum can stay for many a day
and he don't need any money.

--the Highwaymen *The Highwaymen* (1961)
"Big Rock Candy Mountain"
(McClintock/Ives/Fisher/trad.)

The idea of a "summer tour" appealed to the five Clansmen, now college sophomores. It was Steve Trott, through his father, who got the ball rolling. On the morning of October 19, 1959, David H. Trott put in a call to his Procter & Gamble colleague Robert H. Short, an executive responsible for much of P&G's television and radio advertising. The elder Trott immediately followed up his call with a memo:

Here is the information concerning the musical group I spoke to you about this morning (of which my son is a member), which is interested in the possibility of getting resort bookings next summer along the east coast.

There are five boys in this combination, all undergraduates at Wesleyan University… Their name is "The Clansmen" and their specialty is folk music. They are a performing group and not a dance combo.

After describing the group, their material, and their instrumental expertise, the letter continued

They would like very much to audition for an agent who handles east coast summer resort bookings and find out whether they are good enough, and their material is right, for bookings during July and August of 1960. Naturally, they have no idea what to expect from this sort of operation but would hope to make expenses plus some keeping money.

I certainly would appreciate it if you could talk to some people in the agent field during your coming New York trip and suggest a person or company to whom they should write. If anyone you talk with is interested in getting in touch directly with them he can communicate with Stephen Trott, Wesleyan University, Middletown, Connecticut.

Across the bottom of the carbon copy that David Trott sent to his son, he wrote out in his own hand, "Steve—We'll see what happens. –Dad."

Robert Short agreed to help and, true to his word, he made contact with Lewis Titterton, Vice President in charge of Radio and Television Programming at Compton Advertising on Madison Avenue. Short also passed along David Trott's memo, and with that as an introduction, Titterton made some calls.

On October 27, Lewis Titterton wrote directly to Steve Trott at Wesleyan. He hoped that he "could perhaps be of some assistance in exploring the possibilities of your unit obtaining summer employment." Two talent agencies had responded positively to Titterton's enquiries, as he explained in his letter to Steve Trott.

> Mr. Arthur Price of General Artists Corporation… is very insistent that if you are going to be given serious consideration by the bookers who attempt to place musical units, you have to come to New York and audition in front of the bookers. He would be very glad to arrange for such an audition to be held at the General Artists Corporation offices.

Titterton explained that Price had gone on to acknowledge the difficulty that college students might have in getting to GAC auditions during the week (as they were not usually held on weekends) and suggested that they schedule their visit and auditions sometime during the upcoming Thanksgiving break. Titterton then went on to inform Trott that

> Mr. Sol Leon of the William Morris Agency… realizing the probable difficulty of your unit getting to New York in the near future, suggested that you might make an acetate recording at your local radio station in Middletown, and have a few well-grouped pictures taken… However, it is only fair to tell you that literally hundreds of records pour into the offices of the first class bookers and therefore a personal appearance is always desirable.

As Titterton's secretary prepared this letter for mailing, a third booking agency telephoned his office, so a postscript was added, indicating that David Sutton of the Music Corporation of America (MCA) would be happy, along with GAC and William Morris, to audition the five Clansmen "at a mutually agreeable time."

The group was thrilled with the letter. While it may sound like a remarkably generous amount of time to be spent by a busy advertising executive on behalf of an unknown quintet of college kids, Lewis Titterton had often remarked that he found real joy in "attempting to help talented people get a toe-hold." The boys began making plans for a Thanksgiving excursion to the big city and, on November 27, 1959, the five Clansmen drove down to New York. Their first audition was with MCA. David Fisher described the location as one of the City's "many old and funky rehearsal studio buildings." It was not an auspicious beginning. "Three men with dark suits and sunglasses walked in, sat down while we sang four or five songs, got up, and left without saying a word." Their last audition, at William Morris, was little better. "*That's* folk music?" asked one of their hosts. Still, they must have liked what they heard, because they began a heated debate among themselves: on which television shows they should they start booking the group? "But we just want a summer job!" exclaimed Steve Trott.

In between the MCA and William Morris auditions, the five collegians kept an appointment at General Artists Corporation. There the group received its most favorable reception, but they were a little taken aback by the agency's formal response. The by now well-established Kingston Trio and the fledgling Brothers Four were dominating the nationwide College Concert circuit, and the idea of putting another folk group on tour had the executives at GAC seeing dollar signs. They offered the five college sophomores a quarter of a million dollars to leave school at once and go on the road. "This could be big!" they declared. Burnett, Butts, Daniels, Fisher, and Trott weren't so sure.

Before discussions could deteriorate further, the five were approached by a man named Ken Greengrass. He was a very successful Personal Manager. Singer Steve Lawrence was a Greengrass client, along with the irrepressible Eydie Gorme. She had gone to high school with Greengrass and had been a singer in his band, where her future manager played the trumpet. Greengrass had been at GAC on other business when Arthur Price asked him to sit in on the audition. Price was interested in the veteran manager's professional opinion. Ken Greengrass was definitely impressed by what he heard, and he was supportive of the group's desire to remain in school. He suggested they consider a recording contract, and advised that they would need a manager as well as an agent. Greengrass told them that he would like to be their manager. After considerable discussion, the boys agreed, and then returned to Middletown to ponder the situation. There was initially some confusion about the definition of roles, the details of everyone's involvement, and the determination of what might be the best arrangement for all concerned. An exchange of letters between David Trott and Lewis Titterton helped clear up some of the questions. Pertaining to Ken Greengrass, Titterton responded on January 12 to the elder Trott's epistle of December 31 by saying

> The fact that he (Greengrass) was impressed I would say
> has notable significance. Mr. Greengrass is highly thought
> of in his field… A group of no previous professional
> experience or contacts in what is a very highly competitive
> segment of the entertainment industry would, I believe, be
> unwise not to engage a personal manager. If Mr. Greengrass
> is willing to take them on, I believe they are particularly
> fortunate.

As their manager, Ken Greengrass quickly arranged for the group to record a demo record at RCA studios in New York, on 24th Street between 3rd and 4th Avenues. There, in Studio A, the boys recorded every song they knew. When Greengrass asked them if they had any more material, they "reluctantly" (according to Dave Fisher) admitted to a quiet little song they had just added to fill out an hours' program for a recent performance at a Connecticut dinner concert. "Michael" was a traditional 19th century black tune which had originated with Georgia Sea Island slaves. Fisher had arranged it as soft, gentle ballad, with Steve Butts providing a hauntingly effective whistling solo to begin and end the song. With their initial recording session concluded, Greengrass asked them what name he should put on the demo before sending it out.

"We call ourselves the Clansmen," offered Steve Butts. Seeing the stunned look on Greengrass' face, he added, "but with a 'C'! With a 'C'!" Greengrass quickly vetoed the inappropriate title. He advised the boys to come up with new name, and soon. After huddling together for a moment, someone suggested they take their name from the title of an Alfred Noyes poem that Dave Fisher was setting to music for a course at Wesleyan. "Now we're the Highwaymen!" they declared to their manager. Greengrass wasn't happy with that one either, but he decided to let it slide for the moment. It was as the Highwaymen, then, that the group was offered a contract to record on the United Artists label, under the supervision of veteran producer Don Costa. Ken Greengrass followed up with Dave Fisher in a letter dated January 27, 1960:

Dear Dave,

The contracts have been forwarded toi my lawyer's office for perusal. I should have them back in a few days. I will let you know when to come to town to meet with Don Costa.

Meanwhile, keep thinking of a name other than "The Highwaymen", as this doesn't seem to meet with much approval at United Artists.

Give my regards to the boys.

Sincerely,

Ken

The name would never be changed.

*   *   *   *   *   *   *   *

In February of 1960, the newly christened Highwaymen recorded their first LP in the small home studio of Rudy Van Gelder, one of the most famous recording engineers in the history of jazz, at Englewood Cliffs, New Jersey. The well-known venue had been personally selected by the President of United Artists Records, David V. Picker, who attended the Highwaymen session. In addition to Burnett, Butts, Daniels, Fisher, Trott and their instruments, producer Don Costa had brought in a trio of professional session musicians. The group wasn't thrilled to have bassist Jerry Bruno, drummer Joe Jones, and guitarist Bucky Pizzarelli backing them, but Dave Fisher admitted that "they helped keep the beat", and they gave the Highwaymen a more professional sound for the group's initial foray into the big-time.

Their debut album, to be simply titled *The Highwaymen*, featured an eclectic lineup of folk songs, highlighted by solid arrangements with strong group harmonies. Interestingly, despite their origins as the Clansmen with supposedly a number of Irish and Scottish tunes in their repertoire, only one of the cuts on the group's first LP had Celtic roots—the "Irish Work Song", a 19th century Irish-American number sometimes called "Pat Works on the Railway". While there were echoes of Scots-Irish music in "Santiano" and "Greenland Fisheries", these Highwaymen were much more than the Clansmen had ever been.

Three of the songs were in French. "A La Claire Fontaine" featured a solo line by Steve Trott and a nice duet by Trott and Dave Fisher. Echoing harmonies highlighted "Ah Si Mon Moine". Trott and Bob Burnett, with high tenor backing from Fisher, expressively presented "Au Claire De La Lune". A fourth cut was in Spanish. Described in the liner notes as "a traditional South American tone picture of a dance festival held hundreds of years ago in the colorful setting of Bolivia", the song "Carnivalito" had been introduced to the group by Chan Daniels, and he and Trott carried on a delightful back-and-forth dialogue throughout. Dave Fisher's took the solo on "Cindy O Cindy", a song by Bob Barron and Bert Long, which had charted earlier for both the Tarriers and Eddie Fisher, and was returned to its original roots as the Highwaymen's nod to Calypso. Another number, "Big Rock Candy Mountain", came from the collection of Burl Ives. "Greenland Fisheries" was a sea chanty. It featured solo lines by Fisher, Butts, Burnett, and Daniels, while the individual voices of Trott, Burnett, and Fisher stood out on the group's version of the "Irish Work Song". "Sinner Man", "Take This Hammer" (a Chan Daniels tour de force), and "Michael" (solo lines by Butts, Daniels, and

Burnett) all came from African-American tradition. Then there was "Santiano". Sounding the most like a Kingston Trio number, it was chosen by United Artists to be the "A" side of the first Highwaymen single. Much to everyone's surprise, "Michael" was selected by producer Don Costa for the "B" side.

Listening to this album today, it is clear that the Highwaymen were developing a more complex musicianship than the Kingston Trio and harmonies as full as, if not fuller than the Brothers Four. What they lacked at the time, perhaps, was the personality and the edge that groups like the Trio and the Limeliters had in abundance. Younger than the Brothers Four, the five Highwaymen's impressive insistence on prioritizing their college educations also put them at a genuine disadvantage. The kind of year-round concert and club touring that the Brothers Four and the Kingston Trio were able to do gave those groups a special cache that was just not possible for five Wesleyan students who took their continuing scholarly pursuits quite seriously. "The Great Folk Music Scare" had always been, after all, more about live performance than studio recordings (although sales of LPs and 45s certainly played a significant role in that phenomenon). The appeal of live performance is what sets folk music apart from other genres. Concert promoters were scrambling much more than record producers during this time.

In preparation for the LP's release, United Artists sent a professional photographer up to Middletown from Manhattan to take pictures for the album cover. Wearing matching short-sleeved white-with-blue-striped oxford shirts and sporting identical dark trousers, the five sophomores were posed all over the college. The best shot had Daniels and Butts seated on the grass with Burnett kneeling behind them, flanked by Fisher and Trott. Fisher held a banjo, Daniels his charrango, and the others all had guitars. In the background loomed the ivy-covered brick and stone façade of the Wesleyan campus. Both photographer and film returned to New York, and life went on for the young Highwaymen.

Between recording the songs and the release of both the album and the single, almost a full year was to pass. During this time, the Highwaymen attended classes during the week and performed at small but respectable venues (for decent, but unspectacular money) on many weekends. Their other interests—academic, athletic, and social—were also well-served. As sophomores at Wesleyan they got their first taste of controversy and protest, as Wesleyan's chapter of AXP—where it had all begun for them just a year or so before—was expelled from the national fraternity for its local policy of admitting Jewish students. Alpha Chi Rho at Wesleyan was quickly transformed into a new fraternity, which its members—including the five Highwaymen—named EQV. The initials stood for Esse Quam Videre—to be, rather than to seem: a call for authenticity over superficiality—and this Latin name and motto was intended to stand clearly in contrast to traditional Greek houses. EQV was founded on a then progressive policy of non-discrimination. While many mainstream national fraternities, like AXP, still did not allow Jewish and African-American members, there were no such membership restrictions at EQV. This special status would help it attract some of the best, brightest, and most determinedly individualistic among those matriculating each year.

That same spring, the Highwaymen had an experience which would change significantly change their lives. Wesleyan Professor David McAllester, the architect of the University's renowned World Music Program and one of David Fisher's teachers, arranged for the sophomore quintet to be invited to perform at and participate in that year's Indian Neck Folk Festival in Branford, Connecticut. "It was a **seminal** three days," said Steve Butts, "**very** important in our musical and professional development." There, Dave Fisher would later recall, they met many folk musicians, like young Carolyn Hester from Texas, who would remain a lifelong friend. Others included Billy Faier, blues legend Reverend Gary Davis, The New Lost City Ramblers, Dick Rosmini, and Roger Sprung (who would make Steve Butts' banjo). There were ballad singers from the British Isles (from whom the Highwaymen first heard "The Calton Weaver" or "Nancy Whiskey", a Scottish song they would later record), bluegrass bands, and dozens of other performers. It was at the Indian Neck Festival that Sandy Bull and Billy Faier taught Steve Butts how to "frail" the banjo. "We heard live bluegrass for the first time," Butts recalled, "and were astounded by its drive and energy". The Highwaymen were struck by the passion and commitment of these talented folk performers, but the group also realized that they were indeed capable of holding their own in this talented company. "We arrived on a Friday afternoon as nervous outsiders," recounted Steve Butts, "and left, exhausted, on Sunday, determined to learn from and be a part of this exciting movement." The Highwaymen were "warmly received" and "generously supported" by the folk community. Since so many of their newfound friends lived in Greenwich Village, noted Fisher, "it made us want to live there."

As classes came to an end that spring, the quintet finally got to experience, at least somewhat, the singing summer job they had set out to find lo those many months before. Soon it would be time for their junior year.

* * * * * * * *

The popular folk music trend continued across the country in 1960. The three shining stars of the west coast—the Kingston Trio, the Brothers Four, and the Limeliters—continued to pack them in and sell records. The Kingston Trio especially continued to turn out Hot 100 hit singles. Among these was their adaptation of an old Boston campaign song, "Charlie on the M.T.A.", which, in the classic folk tradition, told a story through its detailed lyrics. New on the folk tour scene was another west coast group—the Chad Mitchell Trio—which had come together at Gonzaga University in Spokane, Washington. Unique among folk groups of the time, they did not play instruments, but sang powerful three-part harmonies, backed by musicians such as guitarist Jim McGuinn and banjoist Paul Prestopino. At the Newport Folk Festival that summer, Joan Baez arrived in a hearse, and with her bare feet and her loose black dress setting her apart from other performers there she sang traditional songs like "Barbara Allen" and "All My Trials" in her own special style. With Oscar Brand as Master of Ceremonies, the 1960 Newport Festival featured John Jacob Niles performing "Mattie Groves" while hugging his autoharp, and introduced Bob Gibson and Bob (later Hamilton) Camp to folk audiences for the first time. Other folk artists also came into their own in 1960. Mike Seeger, half-brother of Pete, attracted real interest in his renditions of Southern Mountain Folk tunes with the New Lost City Ramblers. Young John Stewart formed his own version of the Kingston Trio, the Cumberland Three, with his friend John Montgomery and his mentor Gil Robbins. Robbins had been Stewart's music teacher at California's Pomona Catholic High School. After performing with the Robert de Cormier Singers and with Harry Belafonte's back-up group, he joined his former student to sing and play the string bass. The Cumberland Three released a trio of albums in 1960, enjoying some success with their collection of Civil War songs. Another threesome, the Journeymen, began performing that same year, and they became regulars on the Greenwich Village scene. Dick Weissman was an outstanding musician who would have a long and significant impact on folk music, but his two compatriots, John Phillips (who later founded of the Mamas and the Papas) and Scott McKenzie ("Are You Going to San Francisco?") were the ones who would go on to more immediate and and fortune. Like the Brandywine Singers (featuring brothers Rick and Ron Shaw), who also emerged from the collegiate folk scene during this time, the Journeymen had gorgeous harmonies, some success as live performers, and relatively little support on the record charts. The Cumberland Trio (not to be confused with John Stewart's Cumberland Three), the Tripjacks, and the Travellers 3 were among the countless other groups who would eventually attempt to establish themselves on the burgeoning folk scene, with varied results.

While this latest folk revival had begun on the shores of the Pacific, it was in New York City's Greenwich Village that it was finding a permanent home. In 1960, Mike Porco opened Gerdes' Folk City there. Furnished simply with a bar, a small stage, and a handful of tables and chairs, it was definitely a "folk purist" club. Regular acts such as the Weavers, Josh White, and Jean Ritchie would stand aside on Monday "Hoot Nights" ($1 at the door) for newcomers like Judy Collins, Phil Ochs, and Jose Feliciano. In addition to Gerdes, the Gaslight, and the Village Vanguard, clubs and coffee houses with names like Café Flamenco, Café Bizarre, The Bitter End, Café Wha?, Figaro, the Village Gate, the Other End, the

Lion's Head, and the Fat Black Pussycat (formerly the Common) were all places where established folksingers rubbed elbows with aspiring artists. Ramblin' Jack Elliot, Oscar Brand, Ed McCurdy, Mississippi John Hurt, Cisco Houston, Theodore Bikel, Len Chandler, and Jean Ritchie could all be heard at these places. So could comedians like Noel Paul Stookey, Hugh Romney (Wavy Gravy), Richard Pryor, Woody Allen, Bill Cosby, Joan Rivers, and Martin Mull, who all got their start in the Greenwich Village basket houses. And there were even more singers to be discovered there: Tommy Makem and the Clancy Brothers, Fred Neil, Joan Baez, Judy Collins, Phil Ochs, Tom Paxton, Tom Rush, and a young Bob Dylan, who arrived in New York in the cold winter of late 1960 to find his first job at Café Wha? under the wing of Neil, who ran the daytime show there.

Like many young folk musicians, Dylan aspired to a place in the Gaslight Café's evening lineup. He described the place as "a cryptic club" but with a real "mystique" about it. Down a flight of stairs from The Kettle of Fish bar, no booze was allowed, but patrons often brought their bottles in paper bags. The Gaslight featured a rotation of folk regulars, which Bob Dylan recognized as "a closed, drawn circle, tough to get in to." After the show there was always a late-night poker game, and it too had its regulars, among them Noel Stookey, Dave Van Ronk, Len Chandler, Hal Waters, Paul Clayton, Luke Faust, and Ed McCurdy.

Dave Van Ronk warmed up the audience at the Gaslight. From his seat on the stage, Van Ronk noticed that a lot of new people were getting in to the Gaslight and other clubs, albeit as part of the audience. Greenwich Village still had a reputation as a haven for Beat poets and beatniks. "The beatniks hated folk music," said Van Ronk.

Real beats liked cool jazz, bebop, and hard drugs.... But in the eye
of the media, folk music and beatnik were one and the same. So a
lot of people came to the Village to see the beatniks, and ended up
seeing folk music.

And as the folk revival, that "Great Folk Music Scare"—both
Martin Mull and Dave Van Ronk have been credited with coining
that phrase—swept the country, more and more people from
uptown were journeying downtown, to the clubs and cafés of
Greenwich Village.

*   *   *   *   *   *   *   *

Meanwhile, in Middletown, Connecticut, the Highwaymen
were back for their junior year. Individually, each was becoming
more involved in his own particular interests and pastimes. Bob
Burnett was immersed in sports and in student government. Steve
Trott, who would give up his beloved golf in favor of the guitar
and the group, focused on the study of French literature. Dave
Fisher had his music, taking courses in counterpoint, harmonic
theory, and choral conducting. Chan Daniels was becoming
increasingly active in Wesleyan's International Relations Club in
addition to his courseload as a history major. Throughout the
autumn of 1960, Steve Butts was the announcer at home football
games, and he continued to work as an engineer for the campus
radio station. Collectively they remained involved with their
fraternity, and they attended classes, lectures, and labs. They
followed the Presidential campaign as John F. Kennedy defeated
Richard M. Nixon in a very close election. They then scattered for

the Thanksgiving and Christmas vacations, finally returning to Wesleyan for the new year. While the nation awaited the inauguration of a new Chief Executive, the Highwaymen were waiting with varying degrees of patience for the release of their first recordings.

IV

1961

Back on campus after their holiday break, the Highwaymen did not have to wait for long. The LP was released before the end of January. The "look" of the album was a little startling when the boys first saw it. Despite all the photographs taken the previous year, the cover design had only a cut-out picture of the five, superimposed over a confused background featuring a cartoon castle and the group's name as if it had been burnt into a wooden sign. Then, on the reverse side, United Artists demonstrated its lack of confidence in the "Highwaymen" name by including an out-of-place engraving of a 19th century English stage coach, as if hoping that this artwork might somehow "explain" a name United Artists had never wanted in the first place. The liner notes were a little better. "Their agility as musicians and singers," stated the final sentence describing the Highwaymen, "plus their strict adherence to authenticity, assures that the future will, indeed, be a bright one."

Authenticity, at least, there was. With the exception of the three professional session musicians backing the group on their recordings, many of the twelve cuts on the LP met most, if not all, the classic folk criteria. All of them were colloquial, indigenous to a particular region or culture. All but three or four originated in the oral tradition of anonymous folk singing, and even those whose authorship was known ("Au Claire de la Lune", "Cindy O Cindy") or attributed ("Big Rock Candy Mountain") had roots in earlier traditions. In short, many were old. And they were simply structured songs, genuinely recreated (again, excepting the session players) and recognized as belonging to the accepted folk canon. There was no real attempt at commercial or pop polish with this debut album. Even the single which came out of it was only half an attempt at popular success. "Santiano", David Fisher's original version of an old song of the California gold rush, had been selected for the A-side because of its driving, Kingston Trio sounding style. But the choice of "Michael" for the B-side was unusual to say the least, and the five Highwaymen themselves held out slim hope for it.

It seemed as though they were right. Neither the 45 nor the LP charted, and when their one-year contract with United Artists expired in February, it was not renewed. The Highwaymen had been dropped from the United Artists label, and their dreams of recording success were considerably tempered. The boys handled discouragement fairly well. They still could hope, and they had their personal interests and their academic pursuits to keep them occupied. Life, and the Highwaymen, would go on.

*   *   *   *   *   *   *   *

Folk music also persevered, the release of yet one more new folk album out of oh so many causing barely a ripple of impact. Who were the Highwaymen? There were other, more successful folk enterprises in 1961. Harry Belafonte's *At Carnegie Hall* LP was a top forty hit. Fresh from their Newport Folk Festival triumph of the year before, Bob Gibson and Bob Camp recorded a terrific live album in Chicago that spring: *Gibson & Camp at the Gate of the Horn*. Singer Randy Sparks put together a new folk group, the New Christy Minstrels, in 1961. A delightful pair of folksinging comedians—Tom and Dick Smothers—made their television debut in 1961 on the Jack Paar Show. The Smothers Brothers had begun their career two years before at San Francisco's hungry i, following in the footsteps of that old (by "Folk Music Scare" standards) group, the Kingston Trio. The Trio had continued their success despite a lineup change. Dave Guard departed and was replaced by John Stewart, who had disbanded the Cumberland Three. This new Kingston Trio played to standing room only crowds for almost 250 concert dates all across the country during that year alone. And for those who would rather stay home, Oscar Brand brought a new show to radio, *The World of Folk Music*. Sponsored by the Social Security Administration, these fifteen minute programs featured Brand with a single guest artist or group. Two songs by the guests and two songs by Brand would be broken up by lengthy public service announcements on behalf of Social Security. Brand would record some of the guest spots in a studio and some from live concert venues. Brand's theme song—

> I've slung my guitar oe'er my shoulder
> and I've wandered this country around,
> and the tunes that I've heard on my journey
> have sung up a wonderful sound

—with its melody borrowed from that old folk standby "Rosin the Beau", became familiar to listeners all across the country. Through his *World of Folk Music*, Brand was able to reach a much wider audience than his long-running and highly acclaimed *Folk Song Festival* on WNYC.

But not everyone was enamored of folk music, it seems. Certainly not New York City Parks Commissioner Newbold Morris. Washington Square Park in Greenwich Village was a favorite spot for folksingers to gather on weekend afternoons. These informal "hootenannies" attracted college students as well as more traditional "folkies". Len Chandler, while studying for his master's degree at Columbia University, had been among those who had discovered the Washington Square Park venue, and by 1961 he was a fixture on the Greenwich Village folk scene. But according to Morris, many residents of the neighborhood had complained about the noise from "hordes of singers" with their guitars, banjos, bongos, autoharps, flutes and dulcimers. It seemed to Morris that these folk singers and the crowds that joined them to listen and sing along were "littering up Washington Square and trampling the grass." More pointedly, one Manhattan patrolman assigned to Greenwich Village commented that these weekend hootenannies were peopled with "hoodlums, perverts, and communists." During the first week of April, Village coffeehouse proprietors like the Gaslight's John Mitchell had publicly charged the New York City Police Department with attempting to shake them down. Then came the following Sunday, April 9, 1961.

It was the Sunday after Easter. More than a thousand folksingers were gathered in Washington Square Park. At 2:00 in the afternoon, Commissioner Morris ordered police to disperse the crowd. At the fountain in the center of the park, singers linked arms under the warm spring sun and sang "We shall not, we shall not be moved!" The police charged. The melee lasted almost two hours. Hundreds of folksingers were handcuffed and taken away, although only eleven were ultimately charged with disorderly conduct. John Mitchell was among those who led hundreds of others, still singing, to the nearby Judson Memorial Church. The headline in the next day's edition of the *New York Mirror* proclaimed "3000 Beatnik Riot".

It wasn't exactly true, of course. As Dave Van Ronk had noted, "beatniks" were not partial to folk music. This was a very different crowd—short-haired, clean-cut college students and skilled traditional musicians—from what the mainstream media perceived the denizens of Greenwich Village to be. The Rev. Howard Moody, Judson's activist rector, embraced the protesters. A "Right to Sing Committee" was established, and it mounted a legal challenge to Newbold Morris' ban on "park minstrels". Israel Young, founder of the Village's Folklore Center, whose Social Folk group had been singing in Washington Square for over a decade, spoke for the Committee, which was supported by neighboring New York University and by the American Civil Liberties Union. "A park exists for all persons in the city," Izzy Young declared.

Their opposition had supporters as well. Newbold Morris had the backing of the American Legion, the Knights of Columbus, the Holy Name Society, and the local Cub Scouts. Morris was adamant. "The community can have either a beautiful park or it can have a dust bowl," he proclaimed. In response, the Right to Sing Committee held an April 23rd rally in a vacant lot on Thompson Street in the Village. There they sang original songs, including "Newbold Morris is a Grizzly Bear" and "There ain't no Morris in this land." Still, it looked like Morris might win. On May 4th, Justice William Hecht of the New York Supreme Court upheld the Park Commissioner's ban. The Right to Sing Committee read the ban carefully, and noted that it specified the playing of instruments. Three days later, they led more than a thousand folkies and their supporters from the Judson Memorial Church into Washington Square Park, where they sang folk songs a capella, thereby circumventing the ruling and frustrating the police, who could only watch and listen.

New York City Mayor Robert Wagner could recognize a public relations disaster when he saw one. The following week he suspended the ban and ordered folk singing to be permitted in Washington Square Park, "on a controlled basis as a compromise between conflicting uses of the people." The Mayor expressed a conciliatory note when he concluded, "I sincerely hope it works." The Rev. Moody was quick to recognize Wagner's intervention. "I think City Hall has learned about the people," he said. He believed that Mayor Wagner now understood "how hard it is to take away from them such a small and insignificant privilege as singing." Still, Commissioner Morris persisted in arguing his case, and the Right to Sing Committee maintained their legal challenge. Wagner, for his part, declined to intervene further. Judge Hecht's ruling was subsequently overturned on appeal. The folkies had won.

* * * * * * * *

Back in Middletown, the five Highwaymen were only casually aware of the folk singing turmoil to their south. They were moving on with their lives. A star on the Wesleyan track team, Bob Burnett set the college's pole vault record that spring, with a height of 12'

8.25" (they still used a wooden pole). He was also elected Vice President of Wesleyan's Student Body for the following year. Victorious elections came to the Highwaymen in threes, as Chan Daniels would be President of the Wesleyan International Relations Club and Steve Trott would be President of the EQV fraternity when they returned as seniors. Dave Fisher also served the Wesleyan student body, as its Social Chairman, booking and bringing to campus such diverse talents as Duke Ellington, Gerry Mulligan, Dizzy Gillespie, The Four Freshmen, The Tarriers (with Eric Weissberg) and the folk duo of Ewan MacColl and Peggy Seeger.

The five were also making summer plans. David Fisher lined up a job as a counselor at a summer camp in the Rocky Mountains. Steve Trott would return home to teach summer school French at Cincinnati Country Day School, while Daniels would also head to his home, in Argentina. Steve Butts had found himself work as an engineer at WRVR-FM radio in New York. Bob Burnett had perhaps the most interesting summer scheduled—he would travel to Africa with Operation Crossroads, founded in 1957 as a cultural exchange program to provide international travel and service opportunities for college students. Crossroads was described by President Kennedy as "the progenitor of the Peace Corps", and Burnett was eager to begin his assignment: spending a summer in Nigeria learning to make cement blocks and helping to build a community center there. Music was still in their hearts but not much on their minds as their vacation commenced and the Highwaymen headed off to their separate endeavors.

In Greenwich Village, the folk scene continued with groups like the Kingston Trio, the Brothers Four, the Limeliters, and the Journeymen appearing there and across the country. In Ontario,

Canada, the Mariposa Folk Festival made its debut in 1961, where Ian Tyson and Sylvia Fricker, already experienced collaborators from smaller Canadian folk venues, made a tremendous impression as Ian & Sylvia. At that year's Newport Folk Festival, Irish singer Tommy Makem and Joan Baez were chosen the two most promising newcomers on the American folk scene. The "Great Folk Music Scare" had not yet run its course. Somewhere the next great folk music hit was just waiting to be born. Little did anyone suspect that it would come from a then virtually unknown college quintet from Wesleyan University.

Unbeknownst to the five Highwaymen scattered for the summer, an independent distributor from Hartford, Connecticut, "Big Ed" Dinello, had become enamored of the B side from the Highwaymen's 45, and he began promoting "Michael", pushing other distributors and disc jockeys to play the record. Dick Smith, a DJ in Worcester, Massachusetts, also liked the song and began a self-proclaimed crusade on its behalf, playing "Michael" several times daily on his regular show. From New England, "Michael" caught on in Canada, and soon the DJ from a small station in the Dakotas was also promoting the record. Slowly, steadily, "Michael" began to take on momentum.

From his $25 a week position as a broadcast engineer at WRVR in New York, Steve Butts was the first to notice "Michael" break into the Hot 100. "You're at number 78 with a bullet on Billboard," he was informed by the station manager's secretary one day. "What does that mean?" he asked innocently. "You dummy! You have a hit record!" she replied. Butts was also peripherally aware of the song's tremendous success on the Canadian charts. Still, he was very busy.

That summer, WRVR-FM hosted a twelve hour "Folk Music

Hootenanny", also called "A Saturday of Folk Music", broadcast from New York's Riverside Church. The engineer for that folk marathon was young Steve Butts. Pete Seeger, Tom Paxton, Dave Van Ronk (a "gentle giant" in Tom Paxton's description, with "a voice like rusted shrapnel" filled with "subtle ramifications" according to Bob Dylan), Mike Seeger and the New Lost City Ramblers, and Ramblin' Jack Elliott were among the many folk artists who appeared. Of particular interest to Butts that day was the appearance of banjo virtuoso Eric Weissberg. Butts was, by his own admission, "into bluegrass at the time", and Weissberg was one of the founders of the Greenbriar Boys, a New York based bluegrass trio. He had also been a part of the Tarriers. A classically trained musician (much like Billy Faier, who also appeared on the show that day), Weissberg was a graduate of both the University of Wisconsin and the Julliard School of Music. While much-acclaimed for his brilliance on the five-string banjo, Weissberg was also expert on the guitar—both acoustic and pedal steel—as well as the bass, mandolin and fiddle. It was his banjo artistry that fascinated Steve Butts, however, as the young collegian had added that instrument to his repertoire. Weissberg performed that day with Marshall Brickman, an accomplished fiddler and bass player, who would also be with the Tarriers for a time.

More than simply the sum of its parts, this half-day of folk music provided listeners with genuine insight into the modern genre's recent evolution. Earlier folk artists like Ellinor Cook and Richard Dyer-Bennett had taken folk music and, in Steve Butts' words

> used their own training and their own style and their own way of singing to present the material... it was genuinely felt, it's just that they came to it with their

own tradition, rather than the tradition of the people
from whom the music came.

The Weavers had originally begun in that vein, working with orchestra and chorus. "I'm sure," said Butts, "they felt that was the only way they could get the music across in those days." After 1955, however, a serious effort was made—exemplified by the new stripped-down Weavers—to go back and "not only sing the songs,

> but to sing them in more a more authentic, more
> natural, more traditional way…. to recreate the
> actual sounds that you might have heard
> in the 1920s or before.

That day at Riverside Church, this trend was exemplified by, among many others, Mike Seeger and the New Lost City Ramblers performing their versions of "Fair Ellender" and Charlie Poole's "Milwaukee Blues". Still, a new group of classically trained musicians had begun adding a more sophisticated sheen to folk performance, while endeavoring not to lose too much of a song's authenticity. In the lineup that Saturday, performers like Billy Faier and the Weissberg/Brickman combination ably demonstrated that traditional instruments and an old-fashioned edge need not be sacrificed when coupled with complex arrangements featuring key modulation, layered harmony, and performance-oriented presentation. At the WRVR "Folk Music Hootenanny", both the older and newer modern folk trends were well-represented.

Late in the show, a young Bob Dylan was introduced. His twenty-plus minute set featured five songs, with guest appearances from Danny Kalb and Ramblin' Jack Elliott. Still, Dylan spent much of the time trying to fix his harmonica on to the makeshift holder he had improvised from a coat hanger. Dylan's mumbling and fumbling had the audience chuckling, and the announcer at one point filled one long silence with

> ...this gives me a good opportunity to read this little piece
> of paper which they've given me. They've decided that instead
> of me signaling to this fellow over here with six earphones
> on his head, that I'm gonna read the station breaks. So, in case
> you didn't know it, you're listening to folk music all day
> today... and harmonica bending... over Riverside Radio,
> WRVR, 106.7, New York City... Would someone volunteer
> to hold this thing up to Bobby's mouth while he's playing?

The man wearing the six earphones, Steve Butts, was unimpressed. This was the very first time that Bob Dylan had been recorded in New York. "I thought he was a real idiot," Butts remarked.

Two days later, "Michael" topped the charts in several Canadian markets and entered the U.S. top forty. From then on, Steve Butts spent part of his busy day at WRVR tracking the meteoric rise of the Highwaymen's "Michael". It was, after all, his whistling solo which set the mood at the start of the song and then ended it so effectively.

Steve Butts wasn't the only one of the five now assiduously tracking "Michael" up the charts. Every chance he got, Dave Fisher would drive into Denver from the Rocky Mountain summer camp where he served as a counselor, to check on the song's progress. In Cincinnati, Steve Trott watched "Michael" climb to number one on local stations there. "Michael" first hit the top of the chart on a radio station in Burlington, Vermont, but soon it was everywhere. At the end of his summer, Fisher traveled to Trott's home in Cincinnati, and from there the two drove back to Connecticut in early September.

"We kept the radio on the entire way," Fisher remembered. "We couldn't believe it; we had the number one song in the country!"

"Michael" held the top spot for several weeks and spent almost three months in the Top 40, almost a full year in the Hot 100. The Highwaymen were gaining recognition and winning fans across the continent and around the world. In Moscow, Idaho, seven year-old Johann Helton listened to "Michael" on local radio. He was so enamored of the song that he asked his mother to drive him to station KRPL so he could meet the group, not realizing that it was a recording—that the Highwaymen weren't actually there. North of the border, the Canadian success of "Michael" was already assured, and the song had begun to appear on European charts as well.

Upon their return to the Wesleyan campus, the five seniors realized that once again they were the Highwaymen, and this time in the full glare of the national spotlight. Their manager, Ken Greengrass, quickly arranged for new publicity photographs of the group, dressed in plaid shirts and wearing matching vests. Now United Artists wanted them back. The Highwaymen's first single had gained the premier chart position on their label, and their *Highwaymen* LP (a re-release, "with the hit song "Michael") had also entered Billboard's Hot 100 (it would peak at 42 nationally, but charted much higher in several markets). Still, United Artists no longer had the act under contract. UA was forced to sweeten the deal considerably to bring the group back into the fold. While juggling their academic obligations, the Highwaymen went right back into the recording studio. With Don Costa once again at the production helm, they recorded a dozen new songs to be released as a new LP, along with an accompanying 45.

At Wesleyan, the Highwaymen remained involved in the social

scene, despite their crazy schedule. The group would occasionally make the rounds of the various fraternities, sometimes singing "Michael" a half-dozen times in one night. Now that they were so prominent in the public eye, the five young men joined the musician's union, Local 499, in Middletown, Connecticut. Oscar Brand visited the Wesleyan campus to feature the Highwaymen on his *World of Folk Music* program. It was all so sudden, but the group was definitely here to stay.

* * * * * * * *

The folk music community in Greenwich Village could not completely ignore the Highwaymen phenomenon. Bob Dylan, who finally made his Gaslight debut on September 6, just two days after "Michael" hit number one, was certainly aware of their success. While "the classic traditional folk snobs... looked down on anything that smelled of commerciality," said Dylan in his recent autobiography,

> ... they were no threat, so I didn't care about it one way or another. Most of the folk crowd trashed the commercial folk stuff... all that stuff had appealed to me a few years earlier, so I didn't feel the need to put it down. To be fair, there were snobs on the other side too— commercial folk snobs. These kind looked down on the traditional folk singers as being old-fashioned and wrapped in cobwebs.... There wasn't any middle ground and it seemed that everybody was a snob of one kind or another. I tried to keep everything in perspective.

Joan Baez remembered those times in the Village. "Sister mystic and fellow outlaw" was how she described herself alongside Dylan just a year or so later. Although they were both from fairly affluent backgrounds, "we were living out a myth, slumming it together in the Village," she recalled. They would walk "the windy streets" and share "afternoon breakfast on MacDougall Street."

There was, however, a more pragmatic, business side behind the myth. The Gaslight Café where Dylan performed that autumn had changed hands, John Mitchell selling out to Clarence Hood. One story has Mitchell losing the Gaslight to Hood's son-in-law in a poker game. Hood's son, Sam, would run the place, and the Gaslight would continue to be one of New York's premier folk clubs. There was also Gerdes Folk City, of course, where Dylan appeared on September 29. These were just the second and third times he was recorded in New York. Yet another Greenwich Village folk venue, the Bitter End, saw the debut of an unashamedly commercial attempt to cash in on the "Great Folk Music Scare". With the Highwaymen on the charts, there was increased interest in folk music from the mainstream music industry. Promoter Albert Grossman and producer Milt Okun sought to put together a "super" folk group, with the express purpose of making money off of the folk music phenomenon. After scouting out prospects like Dave Van Ronk and members of the Chad Mitchell Trio, Okun and Grossman settled on three somewhat experienced but relatively unknown performers. Peter Yarrow was a twenty-three year-old guitarist with a psychology degree from Cornell, where he had been one of the earliest Presidents of the Cornell Folk Song Club. Noel Stookey, just twenty-four, was a Greenwich Village veteran as a Gaslight Master of Ceremonies, popular comedian, and folksinger. Twenty-four year-old Mary Travers, born in Kentucky and raised in Greenwich Village, had recorded with Pete Seeger when she was only fourteen, had performed in a Broadway revue, and had been singing with a folk group called the Song Swappers. With Stookey using his middle name, they became Peter, Paul, and Mary. The very first song they ever did together was "Mary Had a Little Lamb", but their repertoire soon expanded. It was at the Bitter End that the Kingston Trio heard them perform Pete Seeger's "Where Have All the Flowers Gone?", which had been inspired by three lines in an old Ukrainian folk song. The Trio immediately offered Peter, Paul, and Mary their song "Lemon Tree" in exchange, and the two groups would record each other's songs, a not uncommon practice in folk circles. Peter, Paul, and Mary would go on to become the most successful and longest-lasting group to emerge from this folk revival, first begun by the Kingston Trio and continued by the Highwaymen.

* * * * * * * *

Time magazine featured the Highwaymen in their October 6 issue that year. "Michael" had sold more than a million records by then, and the five were gearing up for the possibility of a concert tour. It was an interesting article, replete with classic *Time*speak and a couple of glaring errors of fact (Bob Burnett wrote the magazine to correct its assertion that he and his Crossroads compatriots had taught the Nigerians how to make cement blocks. "They taught **us**," he insisted). Still, the article acknowledged the group's prioritizing their academic obligations, and it concluded with a perceptive observation from Chan Daniels. Their folksinging was just "a hobby in overdrive," he said. "But it certainly puts academia in touch with reality."

Reality continued to intrude on their lives when the Highwaymen were the cover feature on the October 7 issue of *Cashbox*. The magazine reported that

> The Highwaymen, one of the most underexposed groups
> ever to hit the Number One Spot on the bestseller charts,
> will finally begin to make the personal appearance circuit
> this Fall... a series of weekend concert dates is now being
> finalized by GAC. The group had disbanded after school
> for summer vacation when their recording of "Michael"
> began its climb. When the finally reassembled, literally
> from the 4 corners of the earth, they had to get settled in
> Wesleyan University, Middletown, Connecticut, before
> planning their future. Their next single is due for release
> by UA in two weeks.

Actually, their next single, a version of "The Gypsy Rover" backed by Dave Fisher's arrangement of Huddie Ledbetter's "Cotton Fields" came out just two days after the *Cashbox* piece, to great acclaim. "The Gypsy Rover"—a song with traditional Irish roots, originally credited to one Leo McQuire on a recording by Arthur Godfrey regular Carmel Quinn, and here arranged by David Fisher—featured a beautiful Fisher solo and another whistling interlude, this time by Steve Trott. It was Oscar Brand who noted that "The Gypsy Rover" turned the classic old love story on its head. Instead of the high-born lady who falls in love with the lowly gypsy, this gypsy turns out to be "the lord of these lands all over". The group had high hopes for this Irish number, which hearkened back to their Clansmen roots. Interestingly, when Fisher first arranged "Cotton Fields" for the group, he thought it was a traditional piece, unattributed. Not even Leadbelly's estate had been aware of "Cotton Fields". A highly charged, energetic folk piece, the song opened with a terrific duet—Fisher in tandem with Chan Daniels. The recording session had been something of a challenge. The Highwaymen had needed eleven takes in the studio to make it exactly right:

"Let's get it this time," Bob Burnett insisted after take ten.

"Fisher and I are vacillating between what verse we're doing," complained Steve Trott.

"We're psychologically hung up on the whole thing," Steve Butts interjected.

"No we're not," Chan Daniels responded.

"We've gotta do it again, come on let's go," said Dave Fisher. "No more of that, you guys."

It was Burnett who had the last word: "This is the last chance."

And they made the most of it. They nailed the song on their next try. The B-side of their second 45, "Cotton Fields" had real pop potential.

That same autumn, the Highwaymen kicked off their first major concert tour as recording "stars" with a show at East Carolina College in Greenville, North Carolina. It was a "tour" that encompassed weekends only, as the five seniors remained quite serious about completing their degrees.

In November, the Highwaymen released their second album. On the jacket of *Standing Room Only* were the five Highwaymen, smiling in their plaid shirts and matching vests. The record brought together another diverse collection of folk songs, but this time there were almost as many attributable, more modern folk pieces as there were traditional folk classics. In addition to "The Gypsy Rover" and "Cotton Fields", both certainly in the former category, the LP featured ten other cuts. "Black Eyed Suzie" was a spicy old bluegrass number from the southern hills of Appalachia, with solo lines by all five Highwaymen. Another old American folk song was "Rise Up Shepherd", a Christmas ballad originally collected by the late Ruth Crawford Seeger, highlighted by Dave Fisher's sweet high tenor. "Three Jolly Rogues" was an old English drinking song, which the group had learned from Richard Dyer Bennett's work. Steve Butts brought to life "The Calton Weaver". Also known as "Nancy Whisky", this old Scottish drinking song had been taught to folksinger Ewan MacColl by his father back in Scotland, and picked up by Butts at the Indian Neck Folk Festival. Another song with Scottish roots was Child Ballad #113, "The Great Silkie", first heard by the Highwaymen from Larry & Myra, and again featuring Fisher's tenor. "Johnny with the Bandy Legs", an amusing love song from South Africa, had been translated from the original Dutch by Josef Marais (of the husband and wife duo Marais and Miranda). The Highwaymen's version is enthusiastic, delightful, and musically complex, with a most catchy echoing chorus.

"Wildwood Flower", like "Black Eyed Suzie" and "Rise Up Shepherd", had its roots in the southern Appalachians. Steve Trott turned this old Carter family song into a solo effort, accompanying himself on the autoharp, which he had first encountered through Mike Seeger and the New Lost City Ramblers. Trott could also be heard on the two Spanish-language songs, brought to the group by Chan Daniels. "Nostalgias Tucumanas" came from a northern province of Daniels' native Argentina, and featured a duet between the two Spanish-speaking Highwaymen. Daniels and Trott were also the mainstays of the lively "Pollerita" from Bolivia, but the song was truly a group effort. Daniels' charrango opened the song and could be heard throughout. Finally, there was "Run, Come See Jerusalem", a modern calypso tune by Blake Alphonso "Blind Blake" Higgs, which told the story of a tragic storm off the coast of the Caribbean. The Highwaymen had first heard the song on a Weavers album, and Chan Daniels rich baritone made it a powerful conclusion to the group's second LP.

Standing Room Only quickly joined the group's first effort on Billboard's Hot 100, while "The Gypsy Rover" began moving up the charts, both in the U.S. and Canada. When that A-side of the Highwaymen's second single was just short of the Top 40, however, DJs began turning the record over, and on Christmas Day 1961, "Cotton Fields" peaked at number thirteen in the United States. In fact, the song would spend even more time in the Top 40 than "Michael" had—a total of thirteen consecutive weeks. With two LPs and a trio of singles on the charts ("Michael" was on its way down, but was still in the Hot 100), the Highwaymen were hustled in to the recording studio during the vacation time to prepare a third album. This one would be called *Encore*.

The Highwaymen's stunning success was international and far ranging. London's *New Musical Express* featured the Highwaymen on the cover of its end-of-year survey edition. On the strength of just a single song, "Michael", the Highwaymen were voted the second most popular vocal group in the world, behind only the far more prolific Everly Brothers, and almost ten thousand votes ahead of the third-place Drifters. More interesting, still, was that the Highwaymen's recording of "Michael" reached the top spot in the UK, well ahead of British-favorite Lonnie Donegan's version of the same song in 1961. "Michael" reached the Number One position in Canada, the British Isles, Australia, Spain, Mexico, South America, France, Italy, and even Japan. Not only among the most successful in record sales around the world, "Michael" was also on the year's Top Ten lists for most-played songs by DJs both in the U.S. and internationally.

*   *   *   *   *   *   *   *

The new Highwaymen album had some company on the folk charts. The Kingston Trio and the Brothers Four had new releases that year, while the Limeliters also put out a critically acclaimed debut album on the Elektra label. Elektra was also the new home of 22-year old Judy Collins who released her first album, *A Maid of Constant Sorrow*, in 1961. But for now, the Highwaymen were getting the lion's share of the attention. The newsletter put out by Izzy Young's Greenwich Village Folklore Center noted the Highwaymen's success, even as it advertised Bob Dylan's first major New York concert, on November 4 at Carnegie Chapter Hall. And an editorial in *TV/Radio Mirror* that December declared

> Watch out, Kingston Trio. These boys (the Highwaymen)
> are liable to ambush you on the road—and they outnumber
> you, too!

V

1962

I'm on my way,

great God I'm on my way.

--the Highwaymen, *Encore* (1962)

"I'm On My Way" (trad./D. Fisher)

With their second big hit song, the Highwaymen were in even greater demand. Theirs was an exhausting schedule. During the week they would attend classes, using all their spare time for rehearsals. Every weekend they would perform three or four shows, all over the country. There were plenty of places now, as folk music had taken off nationwide. There were folk venues everywhere. In San Francisco you could find the hungry i and the Purple Onion. In LA there was the Troubador. Also in California were the Unicorn, the Garrett, and the Ash Grove. Mr. Kelly's and the Gate of the Horn were in Chicago. Philadelphia had the Second Fret and Boston its Club Mt. Auburn 47. The Exodus, the Tarot, the Spider, and the Limelite made Denver a western stop on any national folk tour. Washington DC had its Cellar Door, while Dallas had the House of Seven Sorrows. There were folk clubs in Charleston, South Carolina and in Miami, Florida. Major concert halls and hotels also scheduled folk concerts. And, of course, there was all that Greenwich Village,

New York had to offer. The Highwaymen played everywhere, on college campuses and in concert halls. Each weekend featured a succession of airports and train stations, hired cars and limousines, drafty dressing rooms and hasty suppers, sound checks and the sounds of appreciative applause. Publicity came from all over the music scene. The January 1962 issue of Charlton Publications' *Rock and Roll Songs* included an article entitled "Around the World with The Highwaymen". In it, the group was recognized for their abilities and achievements, particularly noting their penchant for international material, which the writer attributes to their having "been collectively, in about a dozen countries." The article concludes,

> Although our book is entitled *Rock & Roll*, we feel that
> any form of music which enjoys public acceptance should
> be publicized, and judging from the sales of their records,
> you teenagers "dig" this group.

That the five college seniors maintained their status as honors students with of all this acclaim and in the face of their busy recording and performing calendars was a remarkable achievement indeed.

In February of 1962, the Highwaymen came out with another single. The A-side was a Dave Fisher arrangement of an old Civil War-era slave song, "I'm On My Way". The B-side featured Fisher's lead vocals on a traditional Irish ballad about a real highwayman, featuring dark deeds and betrayal, entitled "Whisky in the Jar" (originally called "Gilgarra Mountain" and sometimes known by variations of that name). Both songs were cuts from the group's yet-to-be-released third album, *Encore*. "I'm On My Way" would chart in the early spring, while "Whisky in the Jar" was a critically acclaimed attempt to match the recent U.S. appreciation of Irish folk music, a genre the Highwaymen had enjoyed since their Clansmen days. Groups like Tommy Makem and the Clancy Brothers, the Dubliners, the Chieftains, and the Irish Rovers were finding and would find popular success on this side of the Atlantic, especially in Greenwich Village. The Highwaymen's "Whisky in the Jar", their sixth song to make the charts, was well in that tradition and the group would return to it time and again over the decades to come.

$$* \quad * \quad * \quad * \quad * \quad * \quad * \quad *$$

The Highwaymen were getting plenty of air time in 1962. In early March of that year, "Cotton Fields" was the number one song in the Los Angeles area, according to station KFWB. Over the course of the next week, DJ Dick Biondi at station WLS in Chicago would promote the *Standing Room Only* LP (with a clip from "Black-Eyed Suzie") and would feature "Cotton Fields" prominently on his playlist. Of course, the Highwaymen weren't the only folk artists to experience radio and sales satisfaction in 1962. *The Slightly Fabulous Limeliters* was released and charted on the RCA Victor label. Joan Baez's *Volume Two* LP also made the Top 40. Peter, Paul, and Mary would score their first Top Ten single that year with "If I Had a Hammer", while the Kingston Trio could also be found in the Billboard and Cashbox rankings. Ian & Sylvia, who had been touring under the management of Albert Grossman, released their first LP that year, "House of Cards", on the Vanguard label, to great critical acclaim. A former folk song also did quite well in 1962, as the Tokens scored a hit with "The Lion Sleeps Tonight", their pop-rock version of the Weavers' "Wimoweh". Even a former folk singer had a good year in '62. Burl Ives had reemerged as a country singer, and his recordings of "A Little Bitty Tear", "Call Me Mr. In-Between", and "Funny Way of Laughing" achieved crossover success on both the country and pop charts.

In the middle of all this, Hollywood called on the Highwaymen. Top motion picture composer Elmer Bernstein (in 1962 he already had Academy Award nominated scores for *The Man With the Golden Arm*, *The Magnificent Seven*, and *To Kill A Mockingbird* to his credit) approached the group with an idea for his next film, *Birdman of Alcatraz*. Bernstein had written a folk-style song called "The Bird Man", for which he wanted the Highwaymen to sing the chorus and backing vocals, while the film's star, Burt Lancaster, provided narration. Bernstein came to Wesleyan, where he worked with Dave Fisher on the song. The group then rehearsed and recorded their part (Lancaster recorded his voice-over on the west coast). Hoping to capitalize on the movie's release, United Artists quickly put out "The Bird Man" as a Highwayman single, backed by an old standby from their first album, "Cindy O Cindy". While "Cindy" had a track record on the charts, "Bird Man" had significantly less chart success (although it did fairly well in a few scattered markets). This was in no small part due to the fact that the song never made it on to the final soundtrack of the film. It was a disappointment, but looking back Dave Fisher believed that "it was the right decision. It was a folk song, and the Bernstein score was modern and realistic. It wouldn't have fit"

This was only a minor setback, however. In May of 1962, *Encore* was released. On the cover was a painting of the five performers, adapted by Frank Guana from one of the earlier plaid shirt-and-vest photographs of the group. On the album were thirteen songs, including "Whisky in the Jar" and "I'm On My Way", all produced by Don Costa and Ken Greengrass' GLG Productions for United Artists. Included was the group's first solely instrumental piece. "Eres Alta" was an old Spanish love song which Ronnie Gilbert had arranged for the Weavers. On the *Encore* LP, it became a classical guitar duet by Steve Trott and Dave Fisher. There were four songs in three different languages, including one each in Hebrew and German, and two in Spanish. "Bim Bam" was an old Hebrew folk song from Yehuda Helevi and Sholom Secunda, sung to welcome in the Sabbath. "Die Moorsoldaten" by Johann Esser, Wolfgang Langhaff, and Rudi Goguel told the story of "the peat bog soldiers", prisoners in the Nazi concentration camps forced to dig peat from the marshes. The Highwaymen arrangement by Fisher and Chan Daniels effectively evoked a haunting, powerful mood. Popular South American folk artist Luis Bahamondes was the source of "Fiesta Linda", a song about a Chilean roundup which Chan Daniels had brought back to the group after one of his trips home to Argentina. Daniels and Steve Trott were also joined by their fellow Highwaymen on the exuberant Costello/Ramos number "El Rancho Grande", featuring a wisecracking dialogue between two Mexican charros (cowboys).

Two particularly affecting cuts were modern folk songs. Young Oklahoman folksinger Mike Settle's "Little Boy" was beautifully presented by Dave Fisher, while Trott and Fisher together helped retell the tragic story of a recent Nova Scotia mining disaster in Ewan MacColl and Peggy Seeger's "Ballad of Spring Hill". In addition to those two songs, the voices of all five Highwaymen—but especially Bob Burnett, Daniels, and Trott—were also heard to great advantage on the Fisher arrangement of an early 20th century folk ballad, "Railroad Bill".

Steve Butts had two arrangements on the *Encore* LP. His bluegrass-style adaptation of the Guthrie/Hays "Lonesome Road Blues" ("Oh, I'm goin' down the road feelin' bad...") featured Butts (known as "the Duke") on his Gibson Flathead Mastertone banjo. "Fare Thee O Babe" was another Butts arrangement, played in a two-finger, contrapuntal country blues style. The simple vocals on this gentle, sad song began with Steve Trott and Chan Daniels in a duet and then moved on to solo lines from Daniels, Bob Burnett, and Steve Butts. Dave Fisher's high tenor harmonized beautifully with the four other Highwaymen as they ended the song.

The final cut on the album was a driving rendition of "Mighty Day" (best known to folk audiences as the opening number of almost every Chad Mitchell Trio concert). With its melody taken from an old spiritual, the song tells the story of the terrible Galveston Flood which began on September 8, 1900. In the Highwaymen's version, Dave Fisher, Chan Daniels, Bob Burnett, Steve Trott, and Steve Butts each took a verse in turn, while their voices blended together dramatically on the chorus.

It was that perfect blend of five very different and distinct voices which made the Highwaymen sound unique. "I call it the group's sixth member," said David Fisher. "Or the fifth member, when we're a quartet. There's Chan and Steve and Steve and Bob and me, and then there's one more voice, that extra guy—the Highwaymen. In unison or harmony, we blend together to make a very different sound. I don't know where it comes from. It's just there, all the time, and very special." Nowhere in the Highwaymen's early career is this "sixth voice" more effectively demonstrated than on the *Encore* LP.

* * * * * * * *

On June 3rd, 1962, Bob Burnett, Steve Butts, Chan Daniels, Dave Fisher, and Steve Trott all received their Bachelor of Arts degrees from Wesleyan University. They were certainly more financially secure than most fledging college graduates. "Michael" by this time had surpassed more than two and a half million in sales, and David Fisher's future father-in-law, Wesleyan Professor Hess Haagen noted that each member of the group "had an income far in excess of President Butterfield." The Highwaymen also had their continuing commitments as performers. On June 17, they appeared on the *Ed Sullivan Show*, part of a lineup of guest stars which included Dave Brubeck, Frank Gorshin, Gloria Lyman, and the Hugh Lambert Dancers. Ed Sullivan welcomed them warmly. In their dark suits and neckties, the boys sang "Michael" and "Sinner Man". Still, Dave Fisher's fondest memory of that Ed Sullivan appearance was that "our dressing room overlooked the rest of the theater, where the dancers from the 'Follies Bergere' were sunbathing in the nude." The Highwaymen also were guests on the Johnny Carson Show that June, where they sang "Michael" and "Cotton Fields". They then made concert appearances at the Virginia Beach Convention Center and at Freedomland in New York City before the month was over. Still, things were about to change for the original Highwaymen quintet.

Steve Trott had been accepted at Harvard Law School for the fall, and he announced to the others his decision to leave the group. The remaining Highwaymen took stock and decided to continue with their collective music career for two more years, to see how far things might take them. They said farewell to their friend and partner and began searching for his replacement. Jim McGuinn was playing guitar for Chad Mitchell and rooming with Mike Settle, who had played briefly with the Cumberland Three. On the recommendation of McGuinn, the Highwaymen sought out Gil Robbins. With experience as a music teacher and as a performer with the classically inclined Robert De Cormier Chorale, Robbins' folk credits included stints with the Belafonte Singers and the short-lived Cumberland Three. He had been playing folk music up in Canada. "I was appearing at a coffee house in Montreal," Robbins related,

> when word reached me through the 'folk' grapevine that a group of young men from Wesleyan University were trying to get in touch with me.... To be very frank, I was not at all familiar with their work, "Michael" and "Cotton Fields" excepted, of course. However, at our get acquainted meeting, we discovered many similar attitudes toward the field of folk music. The discovery that made the biggest impression on me was their basic honesty and directness of approach to the music.

Robbins, ten years older than the young Highwaymen, was a skilled, experienced musician, singer and performer, who played guitar, bass, and, later, guitarron (a six-string acoustic bass guitar most often seen in Mariachi bands). By mutual agreement, he and the group underwent a brief trial period. They then decided, in Robbins' own words, "that a permanent association would be artistically satisfying without being too hard on the individual psyches."

The Highwaymen soon relocated to Greenwich Village, where Gil Robbins had moved with his family to become the co-manager of Sam Hood's Gaslight Café. There Robbins would play bass alongside Barry Kornfeld on banjo as they backed up Tom Paxton and his guitar on Paxton's first ever LP, a live album on the short-lived Gaslight label, entitled *I'm the Man Who Built the Bridge*.

Paxton was a regular on the Village folk scene, and soon the Highwaymen would be too, as through Robbins' influence they became the Gaslight's "house band". There wasn't much money in it—that would come from recording and touring—but it gave the group, now embarked on a full-time professional career, the opportunity to make folk connections while trying out new material in front of a live audience. These folk connections included being exposed to a multitude of artists who performed regularly at the Gaslight: Paxton, Van Ronk, Chandler, Phil Ochs, Flip Wilson, Bill Cosby, Chuck and Joni Mitchell, Ramblin' Jack Elliot, Alix Dobkin, Johnny Hammond, Eric Weissberg's Greenbrier Boys, the duo of Felix Papalardi and Lou Gossett, Mississippi John Hurt, David Bromberg, Vince Martin and Fred Neil, David Blue, Buffy St. Marie, Patrick Sky, Spider John Koerner, Bob Dylan, Johnny Cash, Jose Feliciano, and many more.

Trying out new material meant growing and developing as performers themselves. With Gil Robbins on board, the Highwaymen began to polish their act. "Gil taught us so much about stage presence, pacing, and putting on a real show," confirmed David Fisher. "He brought a tremendous amount of professionalism and musicianship to the group." While there had been a solid foundation to build on, Steve Butts agreed with Fisher's assessment of Robbins' impact on the Highwaymen. "He was a professional," Butts declared. "He brought to us the experience and knowledge of someone who had made his living performing the music that we loved."

While settling in to their Greenwich Village routine, the Highwaymen were increasingly aware of and pleased by their international success. "Michael" and "Cotton Fields" continued to sell extremely well throughout the world, and one could find

Highwaymen recordings almost anywhere. Both *The Highwaymen* and *Standing Room Only* did very well as special Australian LPs. A 7" disc released in France featured four Highwaymen selections and had on its sleeve cover one of the original Wesleyan photographs of the group, with the campus clearly visible in the background. In Italy, of all places, "The Bird Man" actually did a reasonable business, but only Burt Lancaster was pictured holding a little bird on the jacket of the 45, "dal film 'L'uomo di Alacatraz'", with no photograph at all of the Highwaymen themselves. At least two different releases of "Michael" backed with "Cotton Fields" came out in Japan. Ironically, it was the new Gil Robbins lineup which appeared on the cover of both. Neither recording, of course, featured Robbins, and Steve Trott, who played and sang on both hit songs, was uncredited. Most intriguing was the successful release in Spain of a 7" disc presenting four songs by *Los Bandoleros*. "Michael" ('Numero 1 en el BILLBOARD'), "Santiano", "Carnavalito", and "Oh, Pecador" ('Oh, sinner man') were the featured cuts, and the reverse side of the sleeve detailed the group's story in Spanish. However, there was no picture of the Highwaymen on the front. Instead, buyers of the record were treated to a close-up of a beautiful woman—lovely, sultry, and blonde. European marketing, of course, had its own rules, and the Highwaymen sold plenty of records in Spain.

*   *   *   *   *   *   *   *

Throughout the summer of 1962, the Highwaymen perfected their act, playing a series of dates in the Village and in Canada (where they appeared on Oscar Brand's *Sing Out!* Television show). This was just a prelude to a lengthy concert tour. Then, in late August, Bob Burnett announced that he had to fulfill his Army Reserve obligation and would be taking a six-month leave of absence. So the Highwaymen went into the studio to record their fourth album, *March On, Brothers!,* as a quartet.

This effort would be supervised by veteran producer Milt Okun, and, overall, it gave the Highwaymen something of a new edge. Several of the songs were Gil Robbins' arrangements of old folk songs, spirituals, and sea chanties under the pseudonym of "Nelson Kramer". Prominent among these was the LP's title track. "March On Brothers!" rousingly re-told the Biblical parable about the man who built his house "upon the sand" while another built his "upon a rock" Robbins' version of the old chanty "Rio Grande", now called "Away, Love Away", was similar to the group's earlier "Santiano". "The Devil's Away was a traditional English tune featuring Gil Robbins' vocal lead and Dave Fisher's soprano recorder solo. The final Robbins-as-Kramer arrangement was "John", an old spiritual, sometimes known as "Walk In Jerusalem", which the Highwaymen performed a capella along with an effective finger- snapping background.

David Fisher brought several arrangements to the new album. "Marianne" a poignant song of longed-for-love, featured a beautiful Fisher/Butts duet. "I'll Fly Away" was Fisher's take on an old slave spiritual, previously adapted by Alfred E. Brumley. The Highwaymen's rendition was loud, fast-paced and driving. In later years, Allison Krauss and Gillian Welch would record their own version of the song. On the Scottish "I Know Where I'm Going", Fisher's "fifth member", that singular blending of individual voices into one perfect Highwaymen sound, took center stage between solo lines from Chan Daniels. Fisher's final arrangement on the LP was a collaboration with Gil Robbins (this time as Gil Rubin) on the Boer War-era "Marching to Pretoria". An exuberant number accompanied by Gil Robbins' twelve-string guitar, "Pretoria" allowed the Highwaymen to shine both individually and collectively.

The one song on the album in another language was Rafael Rossi's "Viva Jujuy", with Daniels and Robbins taking the lead together in exquisite Spanish. Bob Gibson and Bob Camp's "Well, Well, Well" was a tour de force for Gil Robbins, and the LP concluded with a group effort—that "fifth member" again—on "One Man's Hands". This last song came from the combined efforts of Dr. Alex Comfort (later best known for his book *The Joy of Sex*) and Pete Seeger. It was the Highwaymen's first venture into that more progressive, reforming strand in the folk genre that would soon develop into full-fledged protest. All in all, *March On, Brothers!* was a satisfying venture for the newly realigned group.

* * * * * * * *

With their latest studio work behind them, the Highwaymen embarked on a major national tour. It was a grueling venture, but nonetheless gratifying. Seven or eight shows a week playing folk venues, concert halls, hotel ballrooms, TV studios, and even the occasional nightclub: the Highwaymen were a sensational success. The "Great Folk Music Scare" was at its peak, and folk acts were in tremendous demand. Prominent among them, the Highwaymen traveled from airport to airport, city to city, and town to town. Under Robbins' guidance, they mastered professional stage skills, and they started including more comedy and playful banter into their act. The

Highwaymen were developing that special something—call it personality, call it edge—that now saw them on an equal footing with veteran acts like the Kingston Trio and the Limeliters. It wasn't always easy. Tempers were frayed from time to time, but the group's collective vision of what they could achieve would always win out in the end.

That fall, *Esquire* magazine's special "Back-to-College issue" had recognized the Highwaymen as one of the year's "Instant Success" stories. The article, which also noted the achievements of other collegiate "Princes" like actor/playwright Austin C. Pendleton (Yale '61) and Heisman Trophy winner Ernie Davis (Syracuse '62) declared

> The true Prince goes right from college to a fabulous
> job, due to his student activity. Today the campus, tomorrow
> the world.... crowned recently—Homage to these leaders,
> because they knew How To Do It.

About the intrepid members of Wesleyan's Class of 1962, *Esquire* lauded them for "wisely deciding that they had a good thing going for them." One of them, Steve Trott, certainly had a good thing going in September of 1962, when he was married. Chan Daniels took a brief break from his obligations with the Highwaymen to stand up as best man for his college roommate. Harvard Law School would begin for Trott shortly afterward. Still, he would remain in touch with his old friends, following their careers with interest even as he prepared for his future in the real world. And the Highwaymen certainly kept their good thing going, as the group played to packed houses night after night.

While they were on the road, the next Highwaymen 45 was

released. "I Know Where I'm Going" got some good air play, and "Well, Well, Well" was also critically well-received, but neither song charted. It was a tough time nationally, as the Cuban Missile Crisis was at its height. Back in New York at the Gaslight, Sam Hood recalled those tension-filled days. "We'd close early and we sat around the big table," he said. Bob Dylan, Dave Van Ronk, Tom Paxton, Luke Faust and others were there. "Everyone just played music for themselves—with no audience. Those were the best nights."

In November, *March On, Brothers!* came out. The album cover saw the four Highwaymen dressed in formal tuxedoes, standing amid piles of fallen leaves. Fisher and Daniels carried guitars, Steve Butts' crutches had been deftly air-brushed out of the shot, and all of them were smiling. The reverse side of the jacket featured less formal photos of each member, taken at their sound-and-lighting check at New York's Blue Angel club, just before a Highwaymen performance there. Gil Robbins with his twelve-string guitar, Butts with his banjo, Chan Daniels playing his guitar were all in front of the microphones at the Blue Angel. Dave Fisher's more studied pose caught him staring off into the distance, dressed casually in a sweater. The new LP made a positive impression in folk circles, and had an intriguing impact elsewhere. Thanks to their recording the Pete Seeger/Alex Comfort "One Man's Hands", the Highwaymen were listed in *American Opinion*—the John Birch Society's regular publication—in that organization's rankings of dangerous enemies of America.

But *March On Brothers* was responsible for more than the verification of the Highwaymen's folk protest credentials. Much of its music became central to their show on tour, although chart success did not follow. With a new year beginning, the Highwaymen's tour still was doing well. And as the weather grew colder back east, the group headed out to the west coast.

VI

1963

A cup of black coffee, a cold café window,
I'm watching the rain turn to snow.
My past rushes in on the gray winter wind--
memories begin to flow.
I hear the echo of strumming guitars,
the world was our oyster, the songs were the stars.
We sang "Goodnight, Irene"
when the Village was green.

--the Highwaymen, *Still Rowing* (1999)

"When the Village was Green" (D. Fisher/A.B.

Clyde)

As 1963 began, the Highwaymen released their next 45—"I Never Will Marry" backed by "Pretoria". Both cuts were slightly different studio versions than were on the *March On, Brothers* LP. This "Pretoria", in particular, featured a powerful drum in the background, beating a martial rhythm. In addition to acknowledging the critical success of the group's recent recordings, *Cashbox* and *Billboard* both noted that the Highwaymen had been among the Top Ten worldwide as sellers of sheet music in 1962. It is sometimes difficult today to remember that sheet music had been the mainstay of the American music industry well into the recording era, and that piano benches and guitar cases in tens of thousands of homes often held piles of published popular songs. David Fisher's arrangements of "Michael", "Cotton Fields" (now credited to Huddie Ledbetter, with a Fisher arrangement), and Leo McQuire's "Gypsy Rover"—each with a photograph of the five original Highwaymen on its cover—sold extremely well. A larger collection, the *Highwaymen Folk Song Album*, was first issued in late 1962 by Hansen Publications of New York, and, at a cover price of $1.50, it was quite successful over the next year. In addition to "Michael" and "Cotton Fields", it contained Fisher arrangements of "Black-Eyed Suzie", "Greenland Fisheries", "Irish Work Song", "Pollerita", "Rise Up, Shepherd", "Santiano", "Take This Hammer", "Calton Weaver", and "The Great Silkie", along with the Gil Rubin (Gil Robbins)/Fisher "Marching to Pretoria", and the Trott-Butts-Fisher adaptation of "Wildwood Flower". New York's Hollis Music also featured the Highwaymen on the cover of their *Hootenanny Sing!* songbook, alongside the Kingston Trio, the Tarriers, Mike Settle, the New Christy Minstrels, the Brothers Four, the Weavers, Leadbelly, and the Limeliters—all pretty heady company for the recent Wesleyan grads. And the overseas success of American folk music inspired new folk groups all over the world. Dave Fisher's arrangement of "Santiano" became a hit in France for various artists, while as far away as Australia the trio of Mel, Mel, and Julian covered the Highwaymen's "Gypsy Rover" and "Sinner Man" in 1963.

That same year saw U.S. folk records doing well. Joan Baez broke into the Top Ten with her *In Concert* album. Bob Dylan's second LP, *Freewheelin'*, was his first to attain Top 40 status. "Green, Green" by the New Christy Minstrels climbed to number 14, while "Walk Right In", a new single by the Rooftop Singers (led by Erik Darling, formerly of the Tarriers and the Weavers) made the Top 40 in three different categories and became the first folk song by a group to hit Number One on the charts since "Michael". A unique recording, "Dominique" by the Singing Nun proved that folk-style songs could transcend both language and culture. Finally, Peter, Paul, & Mary took two songs—"Puff the Magic Dragon" and Bob Dylan's "Blowin' in the Wind"—all the way up to second place on the charts, and two of their LPs hit the Top Ten. In an interview that year, Peter, Paul, and Mary agreed that the Highwaymen were among their favorite folk groups, because they approached each song for the song's sake and didn't try to make the music fit any particular sound or style.

* * * * * * * *

The Highwaymen continued their extended tour in early 1963 through Colorado, Arizona, Washington, Oregon, and California. In February, Bob Burnett rejoined the group in San Francisco. The Highwaymen were performing at the hungry i on the same bill as Woody Allen when Burnett arrived, having been discharged from his six month Army Reserve obligation. He had followed the fortunes of his friends from afar, listening to the *March On, Brothers!* LP and practicing the guitar whenever he could. He had also found time for a personal life. "I was only a private," he recalled, "not even a PFC. I was dating my commanding officer's daughter—and it wasn't easy!"

Burnett was soon up to speed with his compatriots, and he joined them for the remainder of the tour. The Highwaymen headed back to performance dates all along the eastern seaboard. They had by this time perfected what Steve Butts called "a real two-hour show." In those days, noted Butts, a concert by a commercial folk group like the Highwaymen

> pulled together the traditional music, and the traditional techniques and instrumentation, but it was really geared toward entertainment, and presenting a fully fleshed-out performance.

There were jokes, there was well-rehearsed banter, and there were opportunities for the audience to sing along. "We had certain segments where you sang along," said Butts.

> You didn't want that to happen all the time because you had some subtle things you wanted to do, that you wanted to get out...There seemed to be a great eagerness on the part of the audience to join in... This music was fairly new to a lot of the audiences, that's why it was popular; that's why people came, to hear this new stuff.

New or old, their act was carefully choreographed for maximum effect. There would, for example, be an intermission. As it ended, the lights were dimmed and the stage went pitch dark. All alone, Gil Robbins would appear at center stage, snapping his fingers and would start to sing the opening lines of "John".

> Walk on, brothers, walk in Jerusalem.
> Walk on brothers, walk in Jerusalem.

He would be joined on stage by the Steve Butts, and they were now singing together

> Walk on brothers, walk in Jerusalem.
> Walk in Jerusalem, just like John.

Fingers still snapping, Chan Daniels, Bob Burnett, and Dave Fisher would emerge, singing

I want be ready! I want to be ready!
I want to be ready, to walk in Jerusalem just like John!

A verse powerfully sung by Gil Robbins was then followed by a soaring Dave Fisher solo, all the while accompanied only by the snapping fingers and background harmonies of their three companions. Concerts at places like the Massachusetts Institute of Technology, the Westchester County Center in at New York's White Plains (where the posters advertising the group's appearance at an inter-collegiate Spring Spectacular Talent Show hosted by Iona College still showed only the Gil Robbins quartet, despite Burnett's return) and the Totem Pole Ballroom in Newton, Massachusetts (where a young fan named Wayne Hagstrom approached the Highwaymen in the men's room there to tell Dave Fisher how much he appreciated his singing) all followed the same rigorously rehearsed pattern.

There were, of course, the occasional aberrant moments, many of them amusing, at least in retrospect. At a nighttime concert held on the racetrack of the Mineola, New York State Fair, host Oscar Brand was out front with his guitar while Dave Fisher was walking toward the back of the stage, facing the audience from the infield. Behind him he heard a noise, and turning, he saw a full-sized bull heading toward him. Fisher was running toward his car when the spotlight picked him up. The audience began cheering loudly while Fisher, still carrying his guitar, could feel the bull gaining on him. Just in time he reached the car, dove inside and slammed the door shut.

With the audience, and Brand, laughing and applauding, the bull stared at Fisher through the windshield of the car before being led away by a racetrack employee. "Thank goodness the bull didn't have a key," Fisher remembers thinking. Oscar Brand and his wife would tell and retell that story (with suitable embellishments) over the next forty-plus years.

*   *   *   *   *   *   *   *

By the time the tour ended, the five Highwaymen were all settled in Greenwich Village. Bob Burnett and Steve Butts shared an apartment at the corner of Bleecker and 11th streets. Dave Fisher was just around the corner on Bank Street, having moved there after officially residing some months in Philadelphia. Chan Daniels was in an apartment over near New York University. Gil Robbins lived with his family in a fifth floor walk-up apartment at 21 1/2 King Street, just a few blocks from Washington Square. Robbins continued to manage the Gaslight, where his young son Tim helped out by answering phones and running errands after finishing his schoolwork and fulfilling his altar boy obligations at the nearby Catholic church. Young Tim Robbins would also watch and listen to performers at the Gaslight—Dave van Ronk, Livingston Taylor, Tom Paxton, Cat Stevens, Eric Anderson, Seals and Crofts—along with, of course, the Café's house band: the Highwaymen. Years later, the younger Robbins would remember his father dragging him out of Richard Pryor's show there.

Lower New York was still a center of folk music and cutting edge humor in 1963. There was the old guard. Alan Lomax was still on the scene, holding parties twice a month in his loft apartment on

3rd Street. Doctors, dignitaries, professors, musicologists, and anthropologists were invited to these, where they would hear folk music performed by the likes of Mississippi John Hurt, and even by section gang convicts out on parole from southern prisons. Not more than two miles away, Woody Guthrie lay in a New York City hospital bed, suffering from Huntington's disease. Jean Ritchie continued to play the Village folk clubs, as did many other veteran folk artists, along with Hugh Romney and other long-time Greenwich Village comics. Ed McCurdy was there, writing and singing his classic peace anthem "Last Night I Had the Strangest Dream", and Len Chandler was performing as well. But there were also some relative newcomers performing in the Village. John Sebastian played at the Nite Owl (veteran Fred Neil also performed there). Jerry Rasmussen occasionally opened for the Highwaymen at the Gaslight, and a young Bill Cosby got his start there on the same bill as Burnett, Butts, Daniels, Fisher, and Robbins. Another young folksinger, Phil Ochs got his start at Gerdes Folk City, introduced by MC Gil Turner. Ochs' Woody Guthrie-inspired "Power and Glory" received a tremendous ovation there. Later he would get steady work opening for veteran folksinger John Hammond. Jose Feliciano also performed in the Village at this time. And there were others. It was to Greenwich Village that a young Native American woman came to pursue a life in music. Buffy St. Marie had been born on a Cree Reservation in Saskatchewan, Canada and had been raised in Maine and Massachusetts. She arrived in New York after graduating from college, like the Highwaymen, the previous year. Blessed with a uniquely powerful voice and a keenly perceptive musical sense, she made an immediate impression on those who heard her and met her, especially on the five Highwaymen.

Some things, however, had not changed. There were still late night poker games at Sam Hood's Gaslight Café. Steve Butts was welcomed into the Gaslight's circle of nocturnal card players, including Hood, Dave Van Ronk, Ed McCurdy, Tom Paxton, and sometimes Bob Dylan. As they dealt and bluffed and bet and raised, they talked far into the night: about folk music, current events and issues, and much more. The nights when there was no poker game, the Village-based folk musicians would gather after hours with their guitars to share in the camaraderie of that special place and time. "People would come over to the apartment," Steve Butts remembered,

> and would sing together for hours and hours, well
> into the morning. Whoever lost his voice first would
> have to buy breakfast for everyone.

The Greenwich Village folk community also supported one another, with small loans and places to crash for the night. And they applauded when one of their number—actor Alan Arkin, formerly of The Tarriers, appeared on Broadway in 1963's *Enter, Laughing*, winning a Tony Award for his performance. Sometimes, however, there were more serious, less celebratory episodes. That year, Len Chandler was struck on the head by a pipe-wielding Village resident who had assumed that a black man had to be some kind of mugger. Near death, Chandler was rushed to the hospitals, where doctors held out slim hope. His friends waited and prayed as Chandler underwent a complicated six-hour operation. Even if they could save his life, the surgeons were almost certain that the talented musician would never use his left hand again. They managed, however, to save both his life and the use of his left hand, and Chandler's friends helped take good care of him until he was back on his feet.

* * * * * * * *

Between poker games, meeting new people, making new friends, and becoming fully immersed in the Village scene, the Highwaymen continued to perform. Weeknights at the Gaslight, weekend concerts on the road—all the while the group was growing and maturing as professional musicians and showmen. There were publicity obligations as well. Ken Greengrass arranged for new photographs of the group. Each Highwaymen wore a short-sleeved, collared shirt of a different color. Burnett wore red, Butts a dark purple, Daniels' shirt a light blue, Fisher's a pale green, and Robbins wore yellow. They posed in a variety of configurations—sitting, standing, some of each, with and without instruments—all well-groomed and smiling. The photos from this session would be used time and again over the next year. In addition, they did radio interviews for publicity purposes. While performing at, of all things, a dermatologists' convention at Washington, DC's Shoreham Hotel, the Highwaymen visited the WETA studio there and talked with Dick Cerri, host of that station's *Music Americana* program. This was a busy and successful time for the group.

Emboldened by their live-performance experiences on the road and especially at the Gaslight, the five Highwaymen decided to make their next LP a "live" album. Early that spring, family and friends were invited to New York's Bell Sound Studio. It was a casual, informal party, which included David Fisher's mother and sister and, sitting way in the back, Ed McCurdy, among others. Producer Nick Perito (later Perry Como's musical director) was at the helm. In the real hootenanny spirit, the gathering opened with the group's hearty rendition of Woody Guthrie's "Roll On, Columbia", joined on the chorus by their guests singing along. Oscar Brand's "Raise a Ruckus Tonight" was the show's second number, featuring solo lines by Chan Daniels, Steve Butts, and Bob Burnet. Gil Robbins handled the MC chores, and his mastery of showmanship is apparent. The oldest of the Highwaymen introduced each member of the group, and when he finally got to himself, Dave Fisher's aside—"Our father"—raised a chuckle from the assembled friends and family. The first of two guests, folksinger Mayo Muir, was then welcomed to the front of the room. "We ran into her quite unexpectedly down in the Village," said Robbins, "and we decided we had to sing with her." The song was Dave Fisher's arrangement of "The Old Maid's Song", a sometimes comic, sometimes lonely lament. Ed McCurdy thought it was "charming and refreshing."

Gil Robbins' humorous turn with his arrangement (again under the Nelson Kramer alias) of "Shaggy Dog Songs" was quite well-received, and this was followed by another Robbins' adaptation. Sometimes known as "Portland County Jail", the Highwaymen version was highlighted by Steve Butts' strong solo and was called "The Tale of Michael Flynn". As a change of pace after this crowd-pleaser, Dave Fisher introduced the group's second guest of the afternoon, Ann Morrill. The wife of a Wesleyan biology professor, Morrill had enjoyed singing folk songs with Fisher when he came by to study with her husband, and here they delivered a beautiful duet to Fisher's tasteful arrangement of the sweet and mournful old English tune, "Turtle Dove". The next two songs recorded were old favorites—the Highwaymen's greatest hits—"Michael" and "Cotton Fields". For the first time in a recording, listeners could get a sense of just how the group handled a live audience. "If you know the song, come on—help us sing it," encouraged Dave Fisher on "Michael" after Chan Daniels' solo verse. "Sing it out!" Steve Butts' whistling ending fades away gently, and all of a sudden the group breaks in to "Cotton Fields". This version is faster, more rollicking than the hit studio single, and the energized audience adds a rhythmic clapping accompaniment. Everyone seems to be having a terrific time indeed.

The five Highwaymen and their two guests next joined in on Dick Blakeslee's powerfully eloquent "Passing Through." Like "One Man's Hands" on their previous LP, this song was further evidence of the group's willingness to grow and mature, once again giving expression to the more progressive protest-reform strand in folk music. Dave Fisher takes the first verse, while all seven join in on the chorus. Gil Robbins and Mayo Muir duet in harmony on the second verse, and the performers are then joined by a clapping, singing audience on the chorus. Ann Morrill sings the next verse, and Chan Daniels takes the final stanza with its quite daring message in the depths of the Cold War and at the height of the Civil Rights movement:

> I was at Frank Roosevelt's side
> just awhile before he died;
> he said one thing'll come out of World War Two.
> Yankee, Russian, white or tan
> taught him man is just a man:
> we're all brothers and we're only passing through.

For a change of pace, the next number was an old camp song, "Mister Noah", done as a delightful comic duet between Chan Daniels and Gil Robbins. The audience roared with laughter and applauded enthusiastically at the end.

The Highwaymen then returned to one of their specialties— foreign-languages—with an Italian drinking song, *La Canzone Del Vino*. Gil Robbins had brought the Robert de Cormier arrangement to the group from his time with the de Cormier Singers. An impressive a capella presentation, both stirring and textured in its live setting, the song—with its unusual and intimidating chorus, translated as "Drink or we will kill you!"—proved to be a real crowd pleaser. A Fisher adaptation of a sweet old Scottish lullaby, "Can Ye Sew Cushions", was then beautifully sung by guest Ann Morrill. Bob Burnett and Steve Butts took a break on this one, as Fisher, Chan Daniels, and Gil Robbins provided a lovely, simple accompaniment. This moving performance was followed by the group's second foreign-language number of the day—"Chanson de Chagrin". Based on an 18th century song by Padre Giovanni Battista Martini, its theme had been utilized more than a decade before by composer Aaron Copeland in his Oscar-winning score for the film *The Heiress*. In this Robbins-as-Kramer arrangement, the Highwaymen delivered a moody and textured performance in French. Again, the group's "sixth member" took center stage.

With her baritone ukulele and strong alto voice, Mayo Muir was the star of "One for the Money". The Highwaymen backed her admirably on this song from the talented Travis Edmonson, half of the famed Bud & Travis folk duo. What followed next was something special. The group delivered a delightful and darkly humorous rendition of Shel Silverstein's "You're Always Welcome at Our House." Gil Robbins introduced the song as "sort of an invitation", and Butts and Daniels followed with a pair of amusing solo verses. All five Highwaymen joined in on the rousing chorus, which was followed by a Dave Fisher verse. Bob Burnett joined Fisher in a cleverly contrapuntal duet, and then the group roared into the next chorus. Robbins took the final verse, and after the last chorus he closed out the song, declaring "Come up and see us sometime" over satisfied applause. The show ended with a sing-along reprise of "Roll On, Columbia". The Highwaymen were more than satisfied with the occasion. Gil Robbins and Dave Fisher set about to mixing their newest record.

*　*　*　*　*　*　*　*

While waiting for their new LP to be released, the Highwaymen continued to work out new material at the Gaslight and to perform at a variety of concert and club venues. They also continued their efforts in the recording studio. That singular voice of the collective Highwaymen—the "sixth member"—was in beautiful form when they recorded a new version of an old spiritual, "All My Trials", arranged by David Fisher. It would be released as a single in May, but it didn't get much air time. Because of their upcoming live album, "All My Trials" never found its way on to an LP release, and it would remain a classic "lost single". Other than the Highwaymen, no one seemed to notice.

But folk music was being noticed that spring, particularly by mainstream television. Certainly there were other popular music reviews on TV, from *American Bandstand* to *Shindig* and *Hullabaloo*, all of which occasionally featured folk artists, but still mostly catered to pop and rock n' roll sensibilities. In April of 1963, however, a program devoted exclusively to folk music, *Hootenanny*, made its debut on ABC-TV. Its format was quite simple. Each

Saturday, the show would visit a different campus around the country, where individual folksingers and folk groups would perform before an enthusiastic collegiate audience. The show's theme— "Hootenanny Saturday Night"—became its signature song. Folk music would finally have a weekly showcase to broadcast the genre right into people's homes. *Hootenanny*, however, was not without controversy. From the beginning there were problems. Despite his stature as one of the leading lights of American folk music, Pete Seeger was banned from being a guest on the show by ABC, because of his refusal to testify before HUAC ten years before. When she found this out, Joan Baez refused to go on, as did several other folk performers. Seeger would eventually host his own folk TV show, *Rainbow Quest*. But *Hootenanny* was not about the leftist tradition in folk music anyway: it was about popular appeal and selling air time. More commercial, pop-oriented groups like the New Christy Minstrels were the kind of guests ABC wanted on the show, and many folk artists, including eventually the Highwaymen, lined up to appear.

* * * * * * * *

In June, the live album *Hootenanny with the Highwaymen* was released. On its cover was a full-color photograph of the group along with their two guests, all singing together before the microphones, with the Bell Studio's sound booth behind them and their sympathetic audience seated in the foreground. On the back of the jacket was a black-and-white shot of the five Highwaymen from their most recent professional photo session, along with detailed liner notes by folk veteran Ed McCurdy, author of the classic "Last Night

I Had the Strangest Dream". Obviously impressed by the group, McCurdy described the experience as

> an occasion of some fine, honest singing by people
> who care about what they sing and who bring to
> each song a freshness and joy that, to this somewhat
> jaded ear, is a blessed relief... all the singers on this
> recording bring their own individual feeling and
> respect to this music which is the common heritage
> of us all.

McCurdy certainly accepted that the Highwaymen were legitimate and comfortable participants in the Village folk scene. At one point, when describing the group's Hootenanny rendition of "Michael", McCurdy noted that "the whistle solo is by Steve Butts. I think he whistles nicely. He also plays a good game of poker. (I know!)" McCurdy's write-up eventually concluded

> I thank the Highwaymen for letting me ramble
> on about them. I like them very much indeed.

As welcome as it was, Ed McCurdy's approving imprimatur was not necessary in order for the listener to clearly recognize that this record displayed the very best of the Highwaymen, old and new. There were the comfortable standbys—"Michael" and "Cotton Fields"—of course, and there were songs in other languages. But there was also humor. Five different cuts on the album allowed those folk music fans who had not seen the Highwaymen live to get for the first time a taste of their comic abilities and the more professional showmanship inspired by the presence of Gil Robbins. There was also that new, more socially conscious edge to the group with

"Passing Through". Finally, there was simply the sheer joy of a live performance with an enthusiastic audience singing along. It is, after all, in live performance that folk music really comes to life. So it was no surprise when their *Hootenanny* album found its way on to the Billboard Hot 100 chart, the first Highwaymen LP to do so since *Standing Room Only*.

In order to promote its new album, the group expanded into advertising publicity. One day they found themselves out on Long Island, participating in a photo shoot for a fashion spread intended for *Seventeen* magazine. With their instruments at the ready, the Highwaymen provided a backdrop for models in black evening dresses by Betty Lane, Alamor, and others. When the pictures finally appeared, in the December 1963 issue of *Seventeen*, they found themselves sharing the eight page feature on holiday evening wear with musician Peter Duchin and actors Gary Lockwood, Tony Perkins, and George Hamilton: all secondary props for the lovely young models. The Highwaymen considered the experience to be interesting and even amusing, but they had felt a bit out of place and uncomfortable.

More to their liking, the Highwaymen again performed with Oscar Brand. In an interview which was broadcast on Brand's *World of Folk Music* radio show, the five were introduced by their host as "one of America's top young folk groups." Brand sang the "old song of the poachers of Lincolnshire in England." Then, after reminiscing about his first meeting with the Highwaymen up at Wesleyan, he turned the microphone over to Steve Butts and Gil Robbins, who introduced "Passing Through". This was a somewhat different performance than the *Hootenanny* track. Gil Robbins made the second verse a straight solo, and Steve Butts sang the third verse (which had been taken by guest Ann Morrill at the earlier Bell Sound Studio session). It was interesting that the Highwaymen would choose their newer, edgier, more progressive song to promote the LP. Their second number for Brand was first introduced by Robbins:

> Well, you know, Oscar, we all play instruments,
> several different instruments in fact. So we thought
> it would be appropriate if we did the next song
> without **any** instruments.

"It's an Italian drinking song," Bob Burnett then announced, "called 'Canzone del Vino'." The following a capella performance was yet another example of that wonderful blending Dave Fisher calls their "sixth member"—the collective voice of the Highwaymen. After Brand thanked the group, Gil Robbins and Bob Burnett bid their host farewell. To end the program, Oscar Brand announced that, "as the Highwaymen hit the road, I've got a highwayman song for you," and the show concluded with his rendition of the "Ballad of Jesse James".

* * * * * * * *

That summer, the Highwaymen returned to the studio to record their next LP. Ostensibly produced by manager Ken Greengrass' "GLG Productions" (for Greengrass-Lawrence-Gorme), folk legend Fred Hellerman was the actual in-studio producer. The record is at once the most personal and, in Dave Fisher's opinion, the most professional of the group's studio albums. Its theme was, as much as anything, the group's diversity and the variety of folk music strands which the Highwaymen embraced. Again, Fisher and Robbins mixed the final LP. There were no Highwaymen "hits" recorded, but it was nevertheless a special collection of songs.

Their friend Buffy St. Marie—dating Chan Daniels at the time—had given the group permission to record one of her newest songs, a passionate anti-war piece called "Universal Soldier". The Highwaymen's version was the first-ever recording of this song which was destined to become a classic. "Universal Soldier" would later be a hit for its creator, and it would eventually be covered by a variety of artists. But the Highwaymen were the first to introduce its powerful message to the listening public, and their rendition makes it clear that the group was more than willing to embrace that dynamic protest strand in American folk tradition which was becoming increasingly more expressive in a decade which would long be remembered for the Civil Rights movement and the Vietnam conflict.

At the same recording session for their new LP, the Highwaymen introduced another song which would go on to greatness in the years to come. Ewan MacColl and Peggy Seeger, the songwriting team which had given the Highwaymen the earlier "Ballad of Spring Hill", had written and performed "The First Time Ever I Saw Your Face" in Canada, but this would be the first-ever U.S. release of their beautifully tender love song. For the Highwaymen, the song is performed feelingly by David Fisher in a remarkable solo highlighting his lovely tenor voice. Almost a decade later, the very same song would be a Number One hit for Roberta Flack.

There were older songs: "Work of the Weavers" was a traditional Scottish folk song from the linen mills of Glasgow; "So Fare Ye Well" dated back to the Revolutionary War and featured Steve Butts' banjo to great effect. There were newer songs: Fred Hellerman and

Fran Minkoff's "The Ladybug and the Centipede"; the Highwaymen's exciting version of the Helms-Schorr "Midnight Train". There were three songs featuring languages other than English: a Chan Daniels/Dave Fisher arrangement of the classic Mexican song of courtship and marriage, "La Bamba" (a pop-chart hit for Richie Valens back in the '50s), with Daniels singing the lead; a new version of the Sabbath greeting—"Shabbat Shalom"—composed by Dov Seltzer of the Oraniam Zabar; and, unique to the Highwaymen, an Afro-Cuban song from Haiti—"Ayaman Ibo Lele"—written in a patois slightly related to French. The other cuts were "Abilene"—the old standard rendered in a solo-bluesy style and effectively arranged by Gil Robbins (as Nelson Kramer) for five voices; "Sourwood Mountain"—Dave Fisher's bluegrass arrangement of an old folk melody, which had been first adapted by Kurt Weill as a hoe-down for the play *Down in the Valley*; and another of Robbins' Kramer arrangements—"Poor Old Man"—updating a traditional sea chanty.

* * * * * * * *

After completing their recording of these twelve songs, the Highwaymen returned a regular summer schedule of concert and club dates, along with doing shows at the Gaslight to try out even more material. Much of the world's attention, however, was elsewhere that summer, and folk music was not far from the center of national events. On August 28, 1963, two hundred thousand people in Washington, DC sang "We Shall Overcome" together, led by Joan Baez. Len Chandler performed his version of "Keep Your Eyes on the Prize", with back-up vocals from Baez and Bob Dylan. "Blowin' in the Wind" was sung by Peter, Paul, & Mary. Voices were raised singing "We shall not, we shall not be moved" just as they had in Washington Square Park some two years before, but this time for much higher stakes. Mahalia Jackson sang "Oh, Freedom" with its powerful chorus:

Before I'll be a slave
I'll be buried in my grave
And go home to my Lord and be free.

"Songs," said Dr. Martin Luther King, Jr., "are the soul of a movement." No one would ever forget his speech that day, as he shared his dream with a nation and with the world.

In Washington that week Bob Dylan first heard the story of a local crime: the death of Hattie Carroll, a black hotel maid, at the hands of a wealthy white man in Baltimore earlier that same year. Dylan, like many, was disturbed by the slap-on-the-wrist administered by the court to socialite William Zantzinger—a six-month sentence for manslaughter—and upon returning to New York and to Greenwich Village, he began to dwell on the story and on the inequities of American justice in a nation polarized by race. Picking up his guitar, he began to write a song.

It was an early October afternoon in the Gaslight Café. Steve Butts was there, drinking coffee with Sam Hood and Len Chandler. The latest Highwaymen 45, "Universal Soldier" backed with "I'll Fly Away" (from the *March On, Brothers* LP) had just been released. The choice of Buffy St. Marie's anti-war protest song for a single release had been a bold one for the usually soft-spoken and non-controversial Highwaymen, but times were changing. As the three men sat there, sipping their coffee, Bob Dylan walked in and began unpacking his guitar and harmonica. "Listen to this song," Steve Butts remembered Dylan saying. "I've just written it." Dylan then proceeded to play "The Lonesome Death of Hattie Carroll" for perhaps the very first time in public. Shaken by the song's power—subtly detailed and yet powerfully moving—Steve Butts recognized the song as

> a masterpiece of protest song writing... one of the greatest protest songs ever written... I had to pick myself up off the floor after that one...

Perhaps Butts recalled his earlier opinion of Dylan from 1961, when he called the mumbling, fumbling newcomer "a real idiot". Yet he had heard Dylan perform at the Gaslight since then, and he had definitely revised his opinion. Looking back on that night in the autumn of 1963, Steve Butts had a new perspective on Bob Dylan. "I thought he was a genius," Butts declared, "and that's been my opinion ever since."

Only a couple of days later, the Highwaymen traveled to Southern Methodist University in Dallas, Texas, where they were the featured group on the sixteenth episode of ABC-TV's Hootenanny. The group sang "March On, Brothers" and "I'll Fly Away" (the latter promoting the less controversial side of their latest single), and joined in with the evening's other guests—Theodore Bikel, Bud & Travis, Bob Gibson, Johnny Cash, and clarinetist Pete Fountain—in performing the show's theme song, "Hootenanny Saturday Night".

Back in New York, their new studio LP, now entitled *One More Time!* was released. A colorful photograph from the photo shoot earlier that year was splashed across the front. There was also a brand new Highwaymen logo, designed by illustrator/author Gerry

Olin Greengrass, wife of the group's Personal Manager. This logo, with the group's name shaped into the contours of a guitar, would later be copied and used extensively by the Monkees, but it was original with the Highwaymen. The album's liner notes celebrated the variety of the group's repertoire and the diversity of the quintet's appeal:

This is the sixth album recorded by The Highwaymen.

There are six new songs and six old songs from six
different countries. We invite you again to come along
with The Highwaymen and listen to ONE MORE TIME.

Not many people did, outside of friends and family and fellow musicians who were impressed with the record as a finely crafted effort. Folk releases were not doing as well anywhere. Even the Kingston Trio's sales were beginning to plummet in the fall of 1963. Perhaps the "Great Folk Music Scare" was winding down.

*   *   *   *   *   *   *   *

There still were performances to be enjoyed. On October 26, Bob Dylan sang "The Lonesome Death of Hattie Carroll" to a concert audience at Carnegie Hall. Only three days before he had recorded the song which had so impressed Steve Butts. It would appear on Dylan's *Times They Are A'Changin'* LP. Other individual artists, such as Phil Ochs, were achieving live success as well. Earlier that year at the Newport Folk Festival, Ochs had performed three new protest songs: "Talking Birmingham Jam", the "Ballad of Medgar Evers", and "John Birch Society". Afterwards, Pete Seeger had told

102

Ochs that, he thought that "John Birch Society" was "sophomoric", but he also encouraged the young folksinger to keep doing topical songs. Ochs, who became a good friend of Steve Butts—"he would sleep on my couch from time to time," Butts recalled—would later write one of the best-known of the early 60s anti-war protests: "I Ain't A'Marchin' Anymore". And groups like the New Christy Minstrels, the Limeliters, and the Chad Mitchell Trio (the latter becoming increasingly politicized: "John Birch Society" would become part of their repertoire) would host *Hootenanny* on TV and appear at venues all over the country. The Highwaymen had their schedule of show dates as well. It was still a busy time for folk music.

November 22, 1963—everyone who was around that day remembers exactly where they were, and the Highwaymen were no exception. They were booked to do two concerts in Charleston, West Virginia on November 21 and 22. The second concert was, of course, cancelled, as the assassination of President John F. Kennedy shocked the nation, signaling the end of an era that many felt had just barely begun. Like millions of people around the world, Steve Trott—between classes at Harvard Law School—was stunned by the tragedy. Everywhere, people sat with their attention fixed to their television sets, watching the slow, stately funeral procession and giving way to tears when the slain leader's young son saluted his father's coffin. Nothing else seemed to matter very much. In December, the Highwaymen released another single—"The Tale of Michael Flynn" backed by "Roll On, Columbia"—both live cuts from the *Hootenanny with the Highwaymen* LP. The A-side flirted briefly with the charts.

VII

1964

And down on McDougall the Gaslight was glowing
the music spilled out in the street.
The painters played chess while the poets confessed
and the beer was so amber and sweet.
Something was blowing in the windy night,
complexions were rosy , our future was bright
We rode black limousines
when the Village was green....
...when the Village was green
Camelot was shining.
When the moon was untouched
the clouds had such silver lining...

--the Highwaymen *Still Rowing* (1999)
"When the Village was Green" (D. Fisher/A.B.
Clyde)

On a cold February day in 1964, the Highwaymen returned home—to Wesleyan University. Since their *Hootenanny* LP had charted, the group had been planning another live release. What better spot, thought Burnett, Butts, Daniels, and Fisher, than the place they had graduated from just twenty months before, and Gil

Robbins agreed. So much had happened to them in that year and a half, and now they were back at Middletown, Connecticut. The morning was overcast and grey when producer Bernie Krause (the Weavers' last banjo player) and recording engineer Tory Brainard began setting up their equipment inside the Wesleyan campus chapel. There would be two concerts that day—one early in the afternoon and one later—and the best from both would be collected into the new album. It was to be called, appropriately, *Homecoming!*, and the group had high hopes for its success.

The clouds had moved on by noon, and the first audience, mostly Wesleyan undergraduates, made their way through the clear, crisp winter air to the Chapel, where they took their seats, warmed by the sun streaming in through the stained glass windows. The audience response to the first concert was energetic, with loud applause welcoming Wesleyan's favorite sons back to campus. The next audience was somewhat more subdued, but the five Highwaymen, having taken the measure of the hall and warmed up during the first concert, were in top musical form during the second show.

The group's set list that day had something for everyone. There were a few of the old favorites, among them "Michael" and "Cotton Fields", but only their live cut of Leo McQuire's "Gypsy Rover" from the evening performance made it on to the LP. There was one foreign language song—Gil Robbins' adaptation of "Le Roi des Buveurs", entitled "Bon Soir", which was sung as their farewell number—and several comedic gems, including Robbins' half-minute rendition of "Go tell Aunt Rhody" and another minute of typical Robbins' "Riddles". Their one comic song was a Tom Paxton/Gil Robbins collaboration called "Shotgun Talking Blues", which the crowd found vastly entertaining. The show opened with a rousing rendition of "Standing by the Gate", from an arrangement by Nelson Kramer (Gil Robbins). Steve Butts, the former home game announcer for the Wesleyan Cardinals, then welcomed the audience and advised them not to fall asleep, because "the mikes pick up **everything!**" His joke about the album not being released "until 1985" reflected the Highwaymen's earliest experience as Wesleyan juniors, when their maiden recording effort took so long to come out and everyone was waiting and waiting. The audience chuckled knowingly, but in fact this had not been the group's more recent experience.

"There Comes Alibama", another South African song from the pen of Josef Marais (from whom the Highwaymen's earlier "Johnny with the Bandy Legs" had come) was a crowd-pleaser with its sing-along chorus. Dave Fisher's version of the old mountain tune "Careless Love" was quite beautifully rendered. In a similarly tender vein was "Jenny's Gone and I Don't Care" from Mike Settle and Alan Ribback. "Possum Meat" was another Robbins-as-Kramer" arrangement of an old song from the Appalachian hills. Dave Fisher's version of the old sea chanty "Did You Ever See a Wild Goose" featured gorgeous harmonies and made quite an impression in just a minute-and-a-half.

One of the highlights of the Wesleyan concerts was the Martin Kalmanoff/Atra Baer composition "Brandy is my True Love's Name". The song had been recorded the previous year by fellow United Artists' solo star Gene Pitney, but the Highwaymen's version was crisper, fuller, and more subtly complex. Also impressive was their soaring, show-stopping rendering of the Woody Guthrie/Almanac Singers "The Sinking of the Reuben James". Studio versions of that number and "Bon Soir" had been released on a 45, but unfortunately they would see little commercial success. Finally, near the end of the program there was a song which once again demonstrated the group's maturing social consciousness. Bonnie Dobson's "Morning Dew", the young Canadian songwriter's provocative vision of a "nuclear dawn", was powerfully presented by the Highwaymen. Quite movingly done, it proved to be one of the most effective and affecting cuts on the album.

*   *   *   *   *   *   *   *

Homecoming! would be released in April to a good response from the critics. However, it too failed to chart. With the exception of Peter, Paul, & Mary ("the apotheosis of the sixties folk groups" according to Steve Butts) and an occasional one-hit wonder, folk music was on the wane as a recording phenomenon. While PP&M had three Top 40 LPs and a Top Ten single (Bob Dylan's "Blowin' in the Wind") in 1964, the Kingston Trio was dropped from the Capitol Records label in the late spring of the same year. While the Serendipity Singers released their one and only Top 40 single "Don't Let the Rain Come In", the Weavers were making their final concert appearance, recorded live at Carnegie Hall and featuring the various members of that group both past and present. Two Highwaymen—Steve Butts and Gil Robbins—attended that historic show.

In no small measure, one of the principal reasons for folk music's popular decline was what would come to be known as the "British Invasion". That same February, while the Highwaymen were preparing to record their *Homecoming!* album, the Beatles made their first appearance on the *Ed Sullivan Show*. The response to the four lads from Liverpool had been building for some time, but after this broadcast, it became huge. British rock groups like the Herman's Hermits and the Rolling Stones would soon follow, and they would quickly come to dominate the charts. Over the next three years, no fewer than a dozen Beatles' songs were Number One hits, and ten more by Beatles imitators—both British and American—would also top the charts. Literally hundreds of other songs by the same groups would chart during that same period.

There were, of course, still folk performances. The Newport Folk Festival that year celebrated country, blues, and gospel artists. Jean Ritchie, Doc Watson, Mississippi John Hurt, Hedy West, Tom Ashley, Clint Howard, Fred Price, Maybelle Carter, Sam Hinton, the Georgia Sea Island Singers, and the duos of Brownie McGhee/Sonny Terry and Lester Flatt/Earl Scruggs were among those who graced the Newport stage in 1964. The May 30, 1964 issue of the *Saturday Evening Post* featured on its cover a young Texan with long blonde hair and a dynamic voice— Carolyn Hester. Her appearance at New York's Town Hall resulted in a pair of live albums and an increasingly successful concert career. The Highwaymen, of course, had known her since the Indian Neck Folk Festival in that long-ago spring of 1960. On June 3rd, Phil Ochs appeared at the Gaslight, where he performed his more powerful compositions— "Power and Glory" and "What's That I Hear"—along with "The Highwayman", Ochs' version of the Alfred Noyes poem which had given Wesleyan's Clansmen their new name. Also at the Gaslight, engineer Tory Brainard put extra microphones on the already crowded stage to record a gospel set by the Highwaymen. Three of the numbers recorded were live versions of old Highwaymen songs previously released only as studio cuts: "Well, Well, Well", "John", and "I'll Fly Away". Three were new to the group—"Pharaoh's Army/Old

Time Religion", "One More River", and "Come Down, Gabriel".
The show was warmly received by the Gaslight audience, and the
Highwaymen planned to use some or all of it on their next, as yet
undetermined, album.

*   *   *   *   *   *   *   *

Driving through northern New Jersey late one night, Steve Butts
was listening to an Oscar Brand-hosted program of folk music on
WNYC. Pete Seeger came on, singing a Tom Paxton composition,
and Butts found himself entranced by the song. "I was so moved,"
said Butts

> that I pulled off to the side of the road and turned
> the engine off, so I could hear the song better. I think
> I learned it that night, memorized it, and I knew I wanted
> to sing it.

The song was "Ramblin' Boy", and the Highwaymen did indeed
record it, featuring Steve Butts' affecting solo lead.

The Paxton tune was only one of a number of ballads recorded by
the group in mid-1963. Gil Robbins adapted "Pretty Mary" for the
Highwaymen, and they also recorded "Doney Gal", a song of a
cowboy's love for his horse, which had been arranged by John and
Alan Lomax. For the first time, they took on a show tune—"Nothing
More to Look Forward To" by Richard Adler—from the musical
Kwamina. Still, their gentle performance gave it a folk lilt. Of
course, they weren't the first folk group to cross into the musical
genre. The Brothers Four had already released "Try to Remember"
from the *Fantasticks*. Show tunes also found their way into more

modern music—an early Beatles release was Meredith Wilson's "'Til There Was You", from the *Music Man*—and others would follow.

Robbins also edited and arranged a 16ᵗʰ century madrigal— "April is in My Mistress' Face"—for the Highwaymen to record. The group then tried their hand at "When the World Was Young", a Johnny Mercer song with definite folk-roots. All of these were destined for an upcoming album, but one rather special Highwaymen cut was less fortunate. It was Gil Robbins again who adapted a traditional English air, "Come to the Fair", for the group to record in anticipation of the upcoming 1964 World's Fair in New York. "It was a good song," commented Dave Fisher, "but it was never released."

* * * * * * * *

Despite its popular, profit-making decline, folk music remained an integral part of the national scene in 1964. It was the "Freedom Summer" of the Civil Rights era, and under its director, Bob Cohen, the Mississippi Caravan of Music got underway. Participants included Judy Collins, Phil Ochs, Pete Seeger, Gil Turner, Eric Anderson, and many others. They would travel throughout the South, teaching and singing in Freedom Schools and helping to register voters.

Live performances at folk music venues still drew crowds. In 1964, Greenwich Village's Café Au Go Go put together its own folk group, the Au Go Go Singers, which included young folksingers Richie Furay and Stephen Stills. That same year, the New Christy Minstrels sold out the Troubador in Los Angeles. Still, this was a polished, commercial folk sound that was moving away from its traditional roots. Their recording of "Chim Chim Cheree" from the just-released Disney film *Mary Poppins* did well for the New Christy Minstrels, and they were invited to sing it at the 1964 Academy Awards, where it won the Oscar. A number of fledgling folk musicians, like Stephen Stills' good friend Peter Thorkelson and the young Texan Michael Nesmith, had already moved to the west coast and were looking beyond folk music to folk-rock and blues. Stills and Furay would follow shortly afterward. That year at the Troubador a young David Crosby met Chris Hillman and Roger (formerly Jim) McGuinn, and they decided to join forces as the Byrds. LA clubs like the Troubador and Whisky A Go Go would soon begin to add far more than just folk artists and stand-up comics to their calendar of offerings.

* * * * * * * *

With all that was changing, record labels began trying to shake things up. United Artists insisted on putting the Highwaymen together with a new producer, Jerry Ragovoy—best known for his work with Janis Joplin—who had "a brilliant idea". The result was a 45 on which the Highwaymen sang but did not play instruments. With Barry Cornfeld on banjo, Eric Weissberg on bass, and Jay Berliner—a "great player" according to Dave Fisher—on guitar, the group recorded "Sweet Mama Treetop Tall" backed by "Nellie". The record was released that summer, but Ragovoy's "brilliant idea" would bear no fruit.

On August 16th, the Highwaymen made what was essentially their last television appearance, on the *Ed Sullivan Show*. Della

Reese was also a guest star that evening. The group sang "Standing by the Gate" and "Pretoria", and they were enthusiastically received by the studio audience. Still, it was clear that the Highwaymen's days were numbered. Some consideration was being given to a tour of Japan (folk music always did well there, and the Brothers Four would establish a huge Japanese following over the next three decades and more), but Chan Daniels wanted to go back to school, and the four Wesleyan alumni acknowledged that they were coming to the end of their original two-year post-graduate commitment.

By the time the newest Highwaymen album—*The Spirit & The Flesh*—was released that October, the group had essentially broken up. Still, it was an interesting concept, put together by GLG Productions. "On one side," claimed Dave Fisher's liner notes, the Highwaymen

> have "The Spirit", a selection of seven spirituals... on the
> flip side you'll find six love ballads.

Combining the group's previous live Gaslight recording of Gospel tunes with the six earlier studio songs including "Rambling Boy", the thematic LP—produced and mixed by Highwaymen Fisher and Robbins—had its moments. The Paxton song was probably the best of the ballad side, while the Gospel tracks, with their live audience response, was generally more energized and effective. The album cover featured yet another photograph from the session of the year before, flanked by Durer's *Praying Hands* (for the Spirit) and Rodin's *Le Baiser* (for the flesh). The reverse side of the jacket once again displayed the Highwaymen guitar logo, along with Fisher's notes.

There would be one last recording attempt by at least remnants of the original Highwaymen. David Fisher had rewritten "Michael", making it faster and giving it more of a rocking beat. He also rewrote the words to reflect both the group's experience and the changing trend in folk music toward social relevance.

Michael swept the USA—Hallelujah!
Now we're singin' it a different way—Hallelujah!...

...River is deep, the river is wide—Hallelujah!
Lots of brothers on the other side—Hallelujah!...

...Freedom's flags gonna be unfurled—Hallelujah!
Gonna shake hands all around the world—Hallelujah!

On the record, Fisher (singing lead) was joined by Chan Daniels, along with the Dick Williams' Singers (a mixed-voice pop group led by Andy Williams' brother), and the backing of studio musicians, including Eric Weissberg on the banjo. Don Costa and Ken Greengrass were listed as producers. The B-side of the single was Dave Fisher's arrangement of the early 20th century American tune "Puttin' On the Style", which also had a lively beat.

The new 45 was released in mid-November of 1964, fulfilling the group's United Artists contract, but by then the Highwaymen had definitely gone their separate ways. Steve Butts would be staying in New York City, to attend graduate school at Columbia University. Bob Burnett would attend Harvard Law School. Chan Daniels was considering acting, but he too would end up at Harvard, in the Business School there. His Wesleyan roommate—Steve Trott—had managed to remain in touch with his fellow Highwaymen, following their progress over the past couple of years while attending Harvard himself. Now they were following in his footsteps, heading into the "real world", through graduate school and beyond.

Gil Robbins had the most interesting post-Highwaymen experience. The Eveready Corporation hired him to go on a publicity tour for them—with his family. After some training and preparation, the Robbins clan—Gil, wife Mary, and children Adele 12, Gabrielle 10, David 9, and Tim 7—climbed in to a station wagon provided by Eveready and began a tour of the country. They were billed as the "Cordless Family", and at every stop they would demonstrate battery-powered appliances and gadgets: Eveready batteries, of course. They distributed press handouts, did interviews with newspapers, radio, and television, and each of them would show off another machine-of-the-future. Young Tim, for example, demonstrated a battery-operated piggy bank with a mechanical arm. While driving between various towns and cities (St. Louis, Chicago, Philadelphia and Washington, DC were some of the major stops on "The Summer of '65 Cordless Family Tour"), Mary would take the wheel so Gil could play the guitar, and they all would sing.

Dave Fisher and manager Ken Greengrass—both in New York—thought it just might be possible to keep some manifestation the Highwaymen going, in an attempt to match the rapidly changing trends in American popular music, particularly folk songs. In the autumn of 1964, the British invasion quintet known as the Animals had topped the chart with their bluesy version of an old folk tune, "The House of the Rising Sun". Although not by a folk group, it was indeed a folk song, and, inspired by the newer sounds being heard on the radio, both Fisher and Greengrass thought that there could be life in the old Highwaymen franchise yet.

So David Fisher set out on a quest to find the "new" Highwaymen. Interestingly enough, his search did not focus on the traditional folk meccas on the nation's east and west coasts. Rather, his gaze turned southward, to the heart of folk roots and to the products of academic institutions where folk music was still being taken seriously: places like the University of Florida.

VIII

1964-1966

I'm on a new road, to a new place,
walking up the hill to fortune with the sun upon my face
I'm on a new road to a new place
leaving loneliness and all the rest behind.

--The Highwaymen, *On a New Road (1965)*
"On a New Road" (Linzer/Randell)

The Southern Folklore Quarterly was a scholarly journal edited by Professor Alton C. Morris, a member of the English faculty at the University Florida. Morris was a strong supporter of folk music. "Folksongs," he wrote,

are the unwritten history of a people and will keep alive
the great dramatic moments of our personal and national
life. Unrecorded documents of cultural history they are
memories of the past that college groups all over the land
are revitalizing and preserving for posterity…. The students
at the University of Florida have rediscovered this heritage
and are pridefully… preserving these songs for future
generations. Wherever Florida students have hailed from
… they have brought their songs with them and have
shared them with their fellow students… These songs,
handed down largely from mother to children by oral
transmission, represent a miniature spectrum of the rich
heritage of American folksong.

117

Morris penned these words for the liner notes of a special album of folk songs recorded by University of Florida students in 1963. The year before, large groups of undergraduates had begun to gather around a roaring fire at the University's Florida Union to listen to classmates perform folk songs. The University of Florida's Counselor to Off-Campus Women at the time was Ruth Neal, a graduate of New York University and the Julliard School of Music, who had been a professional folksinger before entering academia. Neal, along with Dr. Morris, encouraged the young performers to record their music, and the result, said Neal, of

> students pressed in cramped concentration around a clearing
> in the carpet only big enough for a couple of guitars and a
> banjo, has furnished ringing evidence that our campus has
> succumbed... to the perennial allure of traditional folk
> melody and lore.

It was this campus atmosphere that nurtured aspiring musicians like Renny Temple and Moses Henry MacNaughten. Temple, the son of a career naval officer, had grown up all over the country, and he was a talented guitarist. MacNaughten was a University of Florida music major who had fronted a twelve-piece rock n' roll band—Moses and the Prophets—as an undergraduate. He played fifteen different instruments and had even performed briefly in New York (after spending one night sleeping in Washington Square Park). After college, he and Temple joined forces with a University of Miami graduate—Roy Cohen—to form the Vikings Three, a folk group featuring Temple and MacNaughten on guitars and Cohen on banjo. Cohen, like MacNaughten a music major, had already played in clubs and concert halls throughout the country. Admittedly inspired by the Kingston Trio and the Highwaymen, they became regulars at a small coffeehouse in Fort Lauderdale, where they shared the stage with musicians like young David Crosby and an up-and-coming comedian named George Carlin.

In late 1964, the Vikings Three went on tour. By this time, Moses Henry MacNaughten had shortened his name to Mose Henry for performing purposes, and Roy Cohen had become Roy Connors. Most of their scheduled dates were in Canada, but they soon began working their way south again. It was in a "beautiful little coffeehouse in Charleston, South Carolina," Mose Henry remembered, that David Fisher found them.

Fisher liked what he heard, and he referred the group to Ken Greengrass. It was Greengrass who offered them a job as three-fourths of a new Highwaymen quartet. They would be joined by Alan Scharf, like Oscar Brand more than two decades before, a graduate of Brooklyn College. Scharf was an actor as well as a singer, with both summer stock and television credits on his resume. The four musicians came to New York, where David Fisher, as their "Musical Director", began to rehearse them in a combination of old Highwaymen songs and new material.

* * * * * * * *

In the March, 1965 issue of *Billboard*, a full page advertisement appeared in the "Music on Campus" section. "Watch out!" it declared. "The Highwaymen are back." Below this banner heading was a photograph of the new quartet—Mose, Alan, Roy, and Renny—wearing matching blazers, their guitars in front of them, framed by a silhouette of the continental United States. The ad listed

David Fisher as the group's Musical Director, under the auspices of General Artists Corporation and the personal management of Ken Greengrass. Interestingly enough, Columbia Records was listed as the new Highwaymen label, despite the fact that they had yet to record, nor had they yet performed in public as the Highwaymen.

Less than a month later, the new group made its television debut, on *Hullabaloo*. The program was hosted that week by Ken Greengrass' marquee client, Steve Lawrence, and also featured as guests something old—the Everly Brothers—and something new— the Kinks. Lawrence helped these fledgling Highwaymen get off to a good start by singing with them on "Cotton Fields", a newer arrangement by Dave Fisher. Later, the group sang "Heaven So High", another Fisher arrangement, this time of an old Spiritual and all the guests joined together on the show's finale, "Downtown." Not long afterward, the four Highwaymen also appeared with Steve Lawrence on the program *Shindig*.

On Thursday, May 6, the Highwaymen were back home in Florida, as the featured group at Dedication Week for the brand new Bayfront Center in St. Petersburg. It was billed as "A Night of Stars" at the Bayfront Center Arena, and they shared the stage with comedian Jonathan Winters, singer Nancy Ames (from TV's *That Was The Week That Was*), and Jack Golly and his orchestra ("the Swinginest Sound in the South"). That appearance kicked off a summer-long nationwide tour of clubs and colleges, from Nevada to Virginia. While playing at the Cellar Door in Washington, DC, Mose Henry holed up in a closet in Fairfax, Virginia to produce the very first song he ever wrote. Ultimately, it would be a collaboration with Renny Temple called "Never a Thought for Tomorrow", which would appear on their new LP.

During this time, there was a growing awareness of the changes in folk music. Old-style acts, like the Limeliters, who by now were as well known for their Coca Cola jingle ("Things go better with Coke!") as they were for their folk songs, were breaking up. New acts, with a very different sound, were emerging. In June of 1965, the Byrds' folk-rock version of Bob Dylan's "Mr. Tambourine Man" was climbing the charts.

In the midst of all their traveling, the new Highwaymen took a twelve-day break to record. In an attempt to keep up with changing tastes in popular music, GLG Productions brought in producer Bob Crewe and arranger/conductor Charlie Calello to run the sessions. It certainly wasn't a folk album. Indeed, the folkiest song on the LP was the Mose Henry/Renny Temple "Never a Thought for Tomorrow". Another Temple original, "I'll Be Gone", had an effective folk-pop sound. Much of the rest of the album certainly reflected Bob Crewe's taste for large, layered production, featuring trombones, violins, drums, piano, and no small amount of electrification. Crewe wrote or co-wrote five of the twelve cuts, and songwriters like L. Russell Brown, Raymond Bloodworth, Neval Nader, Denny Randall, and Sandy Linzer were also amply represented. Conductor Charlie Calello played guitar on the backing tracks and he had a hand in writing one of the songs on the LP. While Dave Fisher was perhaps less-than-pleased with the result, Mose Henry thought it was "just a marvelous experience," and he noted quite accurately that it was "a real change from traditional folk music... more of a soft pop/folk/rock."

The album was released in August, just as the Highwaymen were finishing their summer club tour. Columbia Records was nowhere in sight. Instead, it came out on the ABC-Paramount label. Its title, *On a New Road*, was taken from the LP's opening track, which began with blaring Bob Crewe trombones. The name, of course, had more pointed connotations. Rick Ward's liner notes took great pains to highlight the new group's bona fides—"under the guidance of Dave Fisher (one of the original members, who are now the group's musical director) and the original founder, personal manager Ken Greengrass"—while at the same time celebrating its departure from the past:

> It's a new philosophy, a new approach, a new sound, a new career.... The Highwaymen have spearheaded the trend toward the integration of folk and popular music, called in some circles 'folk rock'... the new sound of the Highwaymen brings together the best elements of folk and popular songs in a step that is an obvious extension of the current trends in music... This departure ... was not based on guesswork. Embarking on a college tour... the four young folksingers sensed a new feeling on campus. The demand for pure folk music had lessened, while an increased interest in the folk-pop style had developed.

Ward went on to praise Crewe's contribution to the album, noting that "he has that intangible 'something' that turns what might have been an ordinary record into a hit." Perhaps, but this time the Crewe magic failed to push *On a New Road* on to the charts, and the singles—the Brown/Bloodworth "Should I Go, Should I Stay" and "Permit to be a Hermit", along with the same duo's "I'll Show You the Way" backed by the original "Never a Thought for Tomorrow"— also went nowhere. While this incarnation of the Highwaymen may have recognized that a change was occurring, that same summer brought the reality of that change home to the folk music world like nothing ever before.

*　*　*　*　*　*　*　*

On July 25, 1965, Bob Dylan took to the stage at the annual Newport Folk Festival, following traditional performances by Bob (Hamilton) Camp and Gordon Lightfoot, among others. Playing an electric guitar, surrounded by amplifiers, and backed by the Paul Butterfield Blues Band, he stunned the audience with his supercharged renditions of "Maggie's Farm" and "Like a Rolling Stone". According to some reports, an outraged Pete Seeger threatened to cut Dylan's power cables with an axe (although Seeger himself would later say that he only wanted to shut off a faulty sound system, which was making it difficult for the audience to hear the words). "You can't do that Pete!" intervened Theodore Bikel, one of the Festival's Board of Directors. "You can't stop the future!"

For the Highwaymen, however, what followed that autumn was more like a step back into the past. They appeared on Oscar Brand's World of Folk Music Program, and sang two unadorned, straightforward folk-style numbers: "Sing Some More" (a Renny Temple composition owing a great deal to both Woody Guthrie and Phil Ochs) and "Never a Thought for Tomorrow" (minus the Bob Crewe sound effects). It was out with the new and in with the old. When the group completed a busy college tour, balancing well-arranged numbers with segments of original comedy, they returned to the studio to record their second album. This one would be arranged and produced by David Fisher, with veteran sound engineer Phil Ramone, under the overall supervision of Ken Greengrass. Although Steve Lawrence was listed as the Executive Producer (GLG Productions stood for Greengrass-Lawrence-Gorme), it was definitely a folk album.

Shel Silverstein's powerful anti-war song "Bright Golden Buttons" was beautifully arranged by Fisher and effectively sung by Mose, Renny, Roy, and Alan (who now used the last name Shaw). Mose Henry was quite proud of that one. Also impressive were Phil Ochs' "What's That I Hear", with its evocative opening

> What's that I hear now ringing in my ear?
> I've heard that sound before.
> What's that I hear now ringing in my ear?
> I hear it more and more.
> It's the sound of freedom calling,
> ringing up to the sky...

and Len Chandler's "Green, Green Rocky Road". There were five cuts written or co-written by members of the group, and the LP ended with Dave Guard's "Bonny Hielan Laddie". All in all, it was a more than respectable effort. Under Fisher's direction, these new Highwaymen had come quite close to mastering the collective sound of the "fifth member". Fisher would later reflect that, if he had known what the future held, he probably wouldn't have put together the second group, but he was very pleased with their second album and proud of some of the arrangements on it.

*   *   *   *   *   *   *   *

While the newest Highwaymen were moving back to a more traditional folk sound, recording the works of established folk artists like Silverstein, Chandler, and Ochs, other folk musicians were moving ahead, hearkening perhaps to the rest of Ochs' lyric:

It's the sound of the old ways falling;
you can hear it if you try...

As far as Phil Ochs was concerned, it was "the light of the old ways a dying" and "the rumble of the old ways a-falling", and not only could this change be heard, but also seen and felt as well. In late 1965, "Eve of Destruction" became the first true protest song to reach Number One on the charts. Sung by former New Christy Minstrel Barry McGuire, it had that real folk-rock sound which resonated with younger listeners. Only a couple of places behind it on the chart was another folk-rock piece—"You Were On My Mind"—from We Five, a new group featuring Mike Stewart, brother of folk veteran John Stewart. We Five also recorded the Dino Valenti/Chet Powers "Let's Get Together", which made the Top 40 two years later as a hit for the Youngbloods. As 1965 turned into 1966, the Byrds topped the charts again, with "Turn! Turn! Turn!". This was a classic piece of folk rock, with lyrics adapted from the Book of Ecclesiates and then set to music by Pete Seeger (who earlier that same year had vowed to end electrified folk music with one swipe of an axe). Other folk-rock songs also charted, including "Ill Never Find Another You" by the Seekers and Dylan's "Like a Rolling Stone". In 1965, John Phillips of the Journeymen and Denny Doherty of Canada's Halifax Three teamed up with Phillips' wife, Michelle, and Doherty's friend, Cass Elliot, to form the Mamas & the Papas. In 1966, their first album—*If You Can't Believe Your Ears and Eyes*—became a Top 40 LP, and they produced hits like "California Dreamin'" and "Monday, Monday". The Mamas & the Papas were the apotheosis of the folk-rock group, combining an electrified sound with soaring, complex harmonies. So many veterans of the early folk scene were moving on.

This was true for those comedians who had shared the Greenwich Village spotlight with groups like the Highwaymen. By 1965, Woody Allen was writing and starring in films. Bill Cosby had moved on to television: *I Spy* made its debut in 1965 and would run successfully for three seasons. Cosby, the first African-American to star in a regular dramatic series, would win three consecutive Emmy Awards as Best Actor.

Of course, some folk music veterans had evolved almost beyond recognition. It was during this period that Burl Ives first appeared as the voice of the Ives-lookalike Sam the Snowman in Rankin & Bass' television production of *Rudolph the Red-Nosed Reindeer*. Ives, once jailed for singing a "bawdy and obscene" folk song and once vilified for naming names at his HUAC appearance, would now forever be immortalized as part of a children's holiday classic.

*   *   *   *   *   *   *   *

In the midst of all this, the new Highwaymen album was released, in February 0f 1966. It was called *Stop! Look! & Listen!* and it seemed to demand that the public take the time to see just how good this new quartet could be. But no one was buying. The group's next two singles—recorded to fulfill their contractual obligations to ABC-Paramount—contained songs that did not appear on any LP. "She's Not There" was fairly ordinary, but it was backed with "Little Bird, Little Bird", from the musical *Man of LaMancha*. It was quite a good recording, impressively arranged by David Fisher and led by Mose Henry's effective solo. Still, the public was not interested in show tunes repackaged as folk music. The next 45—"My Foolish

Pride", backed with "Flame"—was a real departure for the Highwaymen. Its robust pop-rock sound, while interesting, also failed to attract an audience.

There was still plenty of concert work for the group. They appeared at venues like the Doral in Miami and at the Starlight in Reno. But it was clear that the Fisher/Greengrass experiment to extend the Highwaymen franchise was not working out. "My heart was being led in another direction," said Mose Henry, and the others felt similarly. It was not an easy ending. There were some difficult discussions and some hard feelings. But in the end, the Highwaymen just expired. Renny Temple, Roy Connors, and Mose Henry would stay together briefly as Family Album, recording unsuccessfully for Columbia under the auspices of producer Mike Berniker, but by early 1967 they had split up. Still, in different ways all four would remain connected to the entertainment industry. Renny Temple would go on to a steady career as an actor and performer, while Mose Henry would eventually carve out a career as a musician for films and television. Roy Connors went into advertising, all the while keeping his musical skills sharp by playing and singing on over 400 television commercials. Alan Shaw would, after a time, move to Seattle, Washington, where would host an early morning TV show.

Film and television would also beckon David Fisher to the west coast, but he remained in New York for a while. After a brief stint as part of a trio (with Gil Robbins and Steve Butts!), he had been performing a solo act at the Gaslight, and he also recorded a solo album for Columbia, produced by Don Costa. The songs were all love ballads. Columbia, it seems, had just lost Johnny Mathis, one of its biggest stars, and they were grooming the ex-Highwayman to be the next Mathis. "Unfortunately", recalled Fisher, "CBS had a regime change, they hired all new executives, and I was lost in the shuffle." The LP was never released.

During all this, David Fisher kept up his contacts with old places and old friends. Steve Butts was still in New York, at Columbia, doing graduate work. Gil Robbins was back in Greenwich Village with his family. Ian and Sylvia came to Thanksgiving Dinner at the Robbins' apartment, and Tom Paxton was a regular around their kitchen table. It was during this time that Tim Robbins made his performing debut alongside his father on a duet of the protest song "Ink is Black, Page is White". A new generation was emerging.

Back at the Gaslight for a party celebrating owner Sam Hood's birthday, Dave Fisher stayed up late with Arlo Guthrie, who was nervous about his draft physical the following day. In the morning, Len Chandler made sure young Guthrie got to his train. The next afternoon, Fisher was rehearsing at the Gaslight, when he saw a figure at the door. It was Arlo Guthrie, who poked his head in and smiled, saying, "I got out!" He then proceeded to tell Fisher the story of his draft physical the previous day. That story would, of course, evolve into the song "Alice's Restaurant". Thus are legends born.

IX

1967-1975

...drifted apart, and we lost somebody along the way,
Oh I wish that he were still around
to be with us here today.

--The Highwaymen, *Still Rowing* (1999)
"The Glory Years" (D. Fisher/R. Davis/A.B. Clyde)

In 1967, Woody Guthrie died in a New York City hospital, where he had been suffering from Huntington's disease for several years. It was the end of a folk era; the passing of a legend. That same year, his son, Arlo, would release his version of Steve Goodman's "City of New Orleans", a song which was very much in the spirit of his father's legacy.

That June, the Kingston Trio played their farewell show at the hungry i in San Francisco, where they had first kicked off "The Great Folk Music Scare" more than eight years before. "The Great Folk Music Scare" more than eight years before. While that exciting period in American popular music had already ended, and while many of the folk acts it had inspired, like the Highwaymen, had come and gone, this too signaled the end of something special. Still, the folk scene it had reenergized continued on, albeit in a variety of directions. At the Newport Folk Festival that summer, Arlo Guthrie's "Alice's

129

Restaurant", an eighteen-minute musical essay on his adventures with the draft board, his police record for littering, and his philosophical ruminations on war and Thanksgiving created a modern folk music legend. Following the example of solo female artists like Joan Baez and Buffy St. Marie, performers like young Bonnie Raitt (the daughter of Broadway musical star John Raitt), Joni Mitchell, and Melanie began appearing in the Village. Steve Butts would take time off from his doctoral studies in Chinese politics to travel downtown to catch their shows at places like the Gaslight, along with performances by other folk artists, such as Richie Havens, John Sebastian, and Ian & Sylvia (who had recently recorded songwriter Steve Gillette's "Darcy Farrow"). That same year, Judy Collins' recording of Joni Mitchell's "Both Sides Now" made the Billboard charts. On television, former folkie Peter Thorkelsen (now Tork) and former folk-country singer Michael Nesmith were starring as the Monkees, and several of that "pre-fab" group's recordings were topping the charts, including "Daydream Believer", written by veteran folksinger John Stewart. Also on TV, the Smothers Brothers Comedy Hour made its delightfully irreverent debut in 1967. New singing stars like Simon & Garfunkel, their pop sound clearly evolved from folk roots, were arriving on the scene. In 1967, Paul Simon's "Red Rubber Ball" became a hit for the folk-rock band Cyrkle, and that same year Simon & Garfunkel's "Sounds of Silence" appeared on the soundtrack of *The Graduate*. Simon's work on the score for that film would win him a Grammy.

*   *   *   *   *   *   *   *

It was music that drew Dave Fisher out to Los Angeles in the late

'60s. He wasn't the only original member of the Highwaymen out there. After graduating from Harvard Law School in 1965, Steve Trott had become a prosecutor in the LA District Attorney's office: a far cry from his gold record/autoharp days with the Highwaymen. It was a reunion of sorts. By 1969, Dave Fisher was settled in Hollywood. A neighbor, just a couple of doors down, was Wayne Hagstrom, the young fan who had first encountered the Highwaymen in the men's room of the Totem Pole Ballroom just a few years before. Known professionally as A.B. Clyde, he and Fisher soon became friends and musical collaborators. One of the first songs they wrote together was "California Calling", which was recorded by Fisher on the MGM label. "It was picked by all the trades to be a hit," Fisher recalled, but MGM chose not to promote it, despite impressive production values (Don Costa, the original Highwaymen producer, was in charge), an energetically layered sound, a strong melody, sweet harmonies, a catchy chorus, and effective A.B. Clyde lyrics. Still, Fisher and Clyde persisted in their musical partnership, turning their attention to television and films. In keeping with Los Angeles' reputation as a city ruled by the automobile, Fisher remembered that "I never walked to Clyde's house. I always drove. It was less than fifty yards away, and I always drove!"

While driving, Fisher no doubt noticed the air play that Peter, Paul, & Mary was getting in 1969. The last of the great folk groups took Peter Yarrow's passionate "Day Is Done" into the Top 40, and then scored a huge Number One hit with John Denver's "Leavin' On A Jet Plane", with the bulk of that song's success coming from album sales. Commercial entertainment, however, wasn't always so kind to folk music that year. In June, the Smothers Brothers Comedy Hour was cancelled by the network. It had become too "controversial", they said. Earlier, as a guest on the show, Pete Seeger had performed his "Waist Deep in the Big Muddy", a dramatic original song outspoken in its opposition to the Vietnam War. At Bethel, New York, just two months later, a number of performers with folk backgrounds took to the stage for the now- legendary Woodstock Festival. "What we have in mind," declared Hugh Romney, now Wavy Gravy, "is breakfast in bed for 400,000." And artists like Joan Baez, Arlo Guthrie, Richie Havens, John Sebastian, Melanie, and Crosby-Stills-and-Nash were among those who sang and spoke to the almost half-a-million strong enjoying their "breakfast in bed" and much, much more.

More than a few miles to the south, in New York City, Gil Robbins was continuing his performing career, this time as an actor. He appeared in off-Broadway shows like *How to Steal an Election*, and he also joined various road companies. Meanwhile, young Tim Robbins performed in plays at the Theatre for the New City. Steve Butts was still in town, finishing up his PhD. and looking for work "figuring out why one particular Chinese political figure was standing so many feet closer or further away from Chairman Mao than another." Elsewhere, having wrapped up his law degree, Bob Burnett, who had married his former commanding officer's daughter, was beginning a career in banking. Chan Daniels was getting started in the recording industry, working for Capitol Records. The Highwaymen were getting on with their lives, even as one of the most turbulent decades in the nation's history was coming to a close. It had been a decade of great hope and great sadness, of great opportunity and great tragedy, and folk music had been at the heart of it all.

But some things, it seemed, were not to last. In 1970, Peter, Paul, & Mary disbanded. The following year, Sam Hood walked away from the Gaslight Café. That great folk venue, begun by John Mitchell with his late night shovel, was closed forever. It seemed that only solo female folk acts were prospering: Joan Baez recording "The Night They Drove Old Dixie Down" and Melanie with her hit song "Brand New Key" best exemplified this strand of the folk experience, while Joni Mitchell and Carole King would continue it well into the new decade. Still, young male performers like John Denver, who had begun his career with the Chad Mitchell Trio, were also emerging. Denver's unique blend of folk, country, and pop would soon make him a star.

*　*　*　*　*　*　*　*

The early 1970s remained a turbulent time, with the continuation of the Vietnam conflict and the election of 1972, which would plunge the nation into the morass of Watergate. Young Tim Robbins would direct his first play and perform satirical political sketches in the wake of that political scandal. His proud father, Gil, would return to music during this time, first playing with Oscar Brand and then beginning a successful career as a choral arranger and director.

It was in 1972 that Bob Shane reformed the Kingston Trio (with new compatriots Jim Connor and Pat Horine) as the New Kingston Trio, and the idea of an old folk group touring as a popular nostalgia act began to take root. Among those noticing were David Fisher in Hollywood and Chan Daniels at Capitol Records, and they both thought that the Highwaymen just might make a comeback.

Daniels had become quite successful as part of Capitol's A&R department. He had been involved in bringing the European group Blue Swede to the American market through his contacts with EMI

(Blue Swede would score a Number One hit in April of 1974, with their cover of "Hooked on a Feeling"). In March of that year, the head of EMI's export department had offered Daniels and Capitol an album by another European group called Triumvirat. "When we listened to the record for the first time," said Daniels,

> we thought it was one of the best productions of the year. Yet there were certain doubts whether a release could be risked merely on the strength of this assumption. So we sent taped copies of the LP to numerous radio stations to test their reactions—which were awesome.

Subsequently, Daniels helped Trimuvirat take their song "Spartacus" into the Billboard Top 40. So Daniels was operating from a position of strength fueled by success when his old friend, Dave Fisher, approached him. A.B. Clyde had collaborated with Fisher on a song about the Highwaymen in the decade since they topped the charts. "It's a long way down… from Number One" was the refrain, and to record it Daniels arranged for the use of a studio at Capitol and handled the producing chores himself. Joining them was the only other west coast-based member of the group, Steve Trott. The three Highwaymen recorded four songs in that session. Along with "Number #1" (as the Fisher/Clyde piece was formally titled) there was a new update of "Michael", a rocked up version of "Cotton Fields", and another Fisher/Clyde composition, "Old Folk Music (with some Sweet Rock n' Roll)". This last song combined an upbeat, electric sound with clever folk harmonies, and lyrics which seemed to evoke the evolution of 60s folk music into 70s rock.

Only the first two—"Number #1" backed with "Michael"—

appeared on the single, which was released in September of 1974 on the Canadian Orion label. The previous February, the original Highwaymen had reunited for ABC TV's *Great Folk Revival*—a huge televised concert held at the Nassau Coliseum on Long Island, in Uniondale, New York. Among those performing were The Tarriers (with Eric Weissberg, Marshall Brickman, and Al Dana); Eric Weissberg again with Deliverance; the New Kingston Trio; a super folk group with Dave Guard, Mike Settle, and Alex Hassilev; Oscar Brand with Gil Robbins; and the Highwaymen—the original quintet with Bob Burnett, Steve Butts, Chan Daniels, Dave Fisher, and Steve Trott. Jean Ritchie's son played bass for the Highwaymen, who did a few songs, and then called up Gil Robbins to join them. This was the group's first and only appearance as a sextet. Shortly afterward, Steve Trott was promoted to Chief Deputy District Attorney in Los Angeles to head up the Criminal Division there, somewhat curtailing his ability to perform and record. But soon none of that would matter.

In 1975, Chan Daniels fell ill with a lung infection which turned into pneumonia. On August 2nd of that year, he died. His death stunned the surviving Highwaymen. They were deeply saddened by the loss of their friend. For seventeen years he had been a part of their lives, and for a brief, intense period from 1961-1964 he had played an integral role in the folk music phenomenon that was the Highwaymen. Without his voice, could the group ever again hope to recreate the unique sound that Dave Fisher had called their "sixth member"? Fisher would later recall that "it was amazing how important Chan's voice was to the sound of the group, even when he wasn't singing the lead. That velvet, smooth baritone gave a real depth to the other, more light-timbred voices." Steve Butts also recognized this. "More than any single member," he said, "Chan was the key to our 'sound'. We never quite sounded the same after his death."

It was, of course, a personal loss as well. "We had a close friendship," said Steve Trott, remembering his first encounter with Chan Daniels at the Meriden railway station in September of 1958, "both personal and professional, that continued until his death." Daniels and Trott had been college roommates, Daniels had been best man at Trott's wedding, and the two of them had lived in Los Angeles during the last years of Daniels' life. Trott would always remember his friend fondly and with admiration.

> Chan had music in his heart and performing in his soul. He relished the stage and reveled in sharing songs with anyone who cared to listen. He had a special affinity for music that was upbeat and happy, music that celebrated the uplifting and affirming aspects of life. It was this inclination which led him to folk music, which he loved—especially the folk music of Argentina and South America. Not surprisingly, given his personality, he found it challenging to sing anything that was sad or depressing.

"Chan was," acknowledged Steve Butts, "a very strong presence on stage, and he brought a great energy to the performances. I often think of his enjoyment in performing when I'm on stage."

Steve Trott summed it up best: "The words of the chorus of one of our favorite songs remind me of Chan's happy outlook on life's journey, from which he was taken far too soon."

> Where the lemonade springs and the bluebird sings
> On the Big Rock Candy Mountain.

X

1975-1986

So I sent myself to school to study law,
and those Cotton Fields have never seemed so far.
Cut my hair and I got myself some power:
now I work all day just rackin' up billable hours.

--The Highwaymen *In Concert* (2002)
"Number #1" (D. Fisher/A.B. Clyde)

Losses never come along by themselves. In the autumn of 1975, Steve Butts ran into his old friend Phil Ochs on a busy New York street. The two went into a nearby coffee shop, where they reminisced about the old days in the Village and what had happened to them along the intervening years. Six months later, on April 9, 1976, Phil Ochs committed suicide. Drug and alcohol abuse and long-term schizophrenia had finally won out over one of the most brilliant creative talents of the Folk Revival. Shortly after his encounter with his old friend, Butts had departed New York, leaving behind his specialty in Chinese politics to enter academia, becoming an administrator at the University of Wisconsin in Madison. With Bob Burnett settled in Rhode Island, Gil Robbins—well into a successful career as composer and vocal director for television— dividing his time between New York and Connecticut, and Dave Fisher and Steve

Trott out in Los Angeles, the Highwaymen were really and truly scattered across the nation.

Other classic folk groups were finding each other again. In 1976, the original Limeliters got back together for what would become a series of annual reunion concerts. Over the previous decade, Glenn Yarborough had made a name for himself as a solo artist ("Baby the Rain Must Fall"). Alex Hassilev had gone into acting (*The Russians Are Coming! The Russians Are Coming!* alongside former Tarrier Alan Arkin) and followed that with work as a record producer. Lou Gottlieb—the group's arranger, MC, and comic genius (as well as its bass player) — had become the resident "guru" at his own Morningstar Commune ranch in California. Back together, the Limeliters unique signature sound, "making three voices sound like twenty", once again delighted audiences throughout the seventies. In 1978, Peter, Paul, & Mary reunited for an anti-nuclear rally at the Hollywood Bowl. The intervening years had dimmed neither their musical talents nor their passion for social justice, and for the next quarter century they would perform together regularly, sometimes as many as sixty shows a year.

New folk artists were emerging as well during the seventies, in addition to the successes of Carole King and John Denver. Both the New Seekers and the Hillside Singers (featuring Rick and Ron Shaw of the old Brandywine Singers) scored with "I'd Like to Teach the World to Sing (In Perfect Harmony)", the latter in a Coca Cola commercial (shades of the Limeliters). Bill Danoff, who had sung with John Denver at Washington, DC's Cellar Door and who had collaborated with him on the mega-hit "Take Me Home Country Roads", formed the Starland Vocal Band. Their one big hit, "Afternoon Delight", topped the charts in 1976 and went on to earn five Grammy nominations, two Grammy wins, and, ultimately, its niche in the Rock n' Roll Hall of Fame. At about the same time, perhaps one of the most enduring of modern folk songs was written in Maine. David Mallett's "The Garden Song" would go on to be covered by close to two hundred artists, including Pete Seeger and Arlo Guthrie. Even the Muppets would take their shot at

Inch by inch, row by row,
gonna make this garden grow...

Maine also was the birthplace of another new folk phenomenon in 1976. That year, the brother act of Chuck and Steve Romanoff joined forces with Tom Rowe to become Schooner Fare, and every Sunday evening they would pack them in at the Holy Mackerel up in Portland. Their rich harmonies and skillful handling of guitars, banjo, electric bass and pennywhistle helped them build up a strong local following. Down East and Canadian themes populated their songs, which mined the rich veins of maritime and military tradition. Their first album, *Day of the Clipper*, was released in 1978.

While old acts were reuniting and while new performers were appearing on the scene, some folk artists had never stopped. Throughout the seventies, Tom Paxton would continue to perform regularly and to add to his prolific output of original songs. When the folk publication *Sing Out!* First published its songbook *Rise Up Singing* in the 80s, only Woody Guthrie, Pete Seeger, and Malvina Reynolds had more entries as songwriters than Tom Paxton. Singing original songs like "I Can't Help But Wonder (Where I'm Bound)", "The Last Thing On My Mind", "The Marvelous Toy", and Steve Butts' favorite "Rambling Boy", Paxton toured a great deal, once memorably through the British Isles with Carolyn Hester and her husband David Blume. Paxton also recorded, and newer artists like the versatile Cindy Mangsen would be recruited to sing backup and harmony on his releases. Two other veterans of the 60s folk scene had also continued creating, but in a different field. Former folk club stand-up comedian Woody Allen had been writing movies with former folksinger Marshall Brickman (The Tarriers), and in 1977 their screenplay for *Annie Hall* won an Academy Award. Folkies, it seemed, were everywhere, sometimes above the radar, more often below it, and only rarely—like Allen and Brickman—right in the public eye.

Two huge folk reunions, however, were the center of attention as the decade of the 1980s began. In November of 1980, the Weavers— the original Weavers: Pete Seeger, Fred Hellerman, Ronnie Gilbert, and an ailing Lee Hays—united for a pair of concerts at Carnegie Hall. Once again, the story of this both seminal and controversial group was told, and a powerful documentary film—*The Weavers: Wasn't That a Time*—emerged from this experience to inform and instruct a whole new generation. The following summer, Lee Hays was dead, signaling an end to the thirty-year run of the century's first and greatest popular folk group.

If the Weavers had been the grandparents of all modern folk groups (and the Almanac Singers the great-grandparents), then the Kingston Trio had fathered the folk revival that exploded on the scene culminating in "Great Folk Music Scare". In 1981, Public Television broadcast a Kingston Trio reunion concert which gathered together all the original members of the group, along with John Stewart and Bob Shane's current lineup. With Mary Travers of Peter, Paul, & Mary as a special guest, this historic production once again brought classic folk-revival/"folk scare" music into the public eye.

But while the Kingston Trio enjoyed being honored as the fathers of the folk revival, among their children the Limeliters decided to make their annual get-together more regular and permanent. At least, two of them did. While Glenn Yarborough wanted to continue his solo career, Lou Gottlieb and Alex Hassilev teamed with tenor Red Grammer to create a new configuration of Limeliters. They would perform together for eight years, appearing at a variety of concert venues and releasing five albums, two of them live. Grammer's own composition—"Harmony"—would become a Limeliter staple, and has rightly earned its reputation as one of the best audience participation songs of all time.

*   *   *   *   *   *   *   *

Among the Kingston Trio's other folk "children", the original Highwaymen were continuing their own careers. Only David Fisher remained in the music business, composing for movies and television in Los Angeles. Lawyer and banker Bob Burnett in Rhode Island and college administrator and academic Steve Butts out in Wisconsin had their own lives, away from the hectic bustle of their performing days. Steve Trott's life, on the other hand, seemed to be getting more hectic. In 1981, he became a Federal prosecutor, when he was appointed the United States Attorney for the Central District of California. The following year, Trott received a promotion, to Assistant Attorney General, Criminal Division, at the Department of Justice, and he began a series of successful prosecutions against organized crime.

Some Highwaymen also found time to reunite, albeit briefly. At the Wesleyan University Class of 1962 20th reunion in 1982, Dave

Fisher was a featured performer. Near the end of his set, he called Bob Burnett up from the audience, and together they did their best to stir up some of the old memories in song.

Despite its obvious appeal to audiences of all ages, folk music was no longer a nationwide popular phenomenon. Commercially, the 1980s favored disco, glam rock, and heavy metal as the decade progressed. But it was a 1982 conversation between Tom Paxton and Washington, DC-based radio host Dick Cerri which would give folk music its first real advocate on the national scene (and, indeed, around the world). The World Folk Music Association was established by Cerri and Paxton in 1983,

> dedicated to promoting contemporary and traditional folk music, spreading the word to fans, and keeping the folk community informed and involved.

With the regular publication of their newsletter, *FOLK NEWS*, the WFMA was well on its way to fulfilling its mission.

* * * * * * * *

It was in 1985 that a country album was released by a band calling itself "The Highwaymen". This would raise some eyebrows in Wisconsin, Rhode Island, California, and even in New York (where Ken Greengrass still plied his trade as a personal manager) because these "Highwaymen" were not Burnett, Butts, Fisher, and Trott, but Cash, Jennings, Kristofferson, and Nelson. Four country music superstars had combined to form a country supergroup, calling themselves "The Highwaymen". Over the next few years, albums by these new "Highwaymen": would do well, but the four originals were not pleased that their name had been "stolen". Were the original Highwaymen even a recognized part of the folk music scene anymore?

Well, others certainly still were. The World Folk Music Association held its first Annual Benefit Concert Weekend in late January of 1986. Among the performers appearing at that seminal event was a talented singer-songwriter from California—Kate Wolf—who less than a year later would die, tragically young, from leukemia. The following year, when the WFMA Benefit Concert was held on Valentine's Day, Dick Cerri and the World Folk Music Association established the Kate Wolf Award, in her memory, "to the performer who best epitomizes the music and spirit of Kate Wolf." Also performing at the first-ever WFMA Benefit were Schooner Fare, Bob Gibson, and the original Chad Mitchell Trio, reunited after twenty years.

At their 25th Reunion at Wesleyan, the four surviving original Highwaymen were finally together again, on stage for a pair of concerts. They played "Michael", "Cotton Fields", and plenty of old favorites, and their take on the decades since their gold record successes—"Number #1"—was particularly well-received. Steve Trott was thrilled when a claque of college girls, screaming enthusiastically, rushed the stage. It was just like old times, he thought, until he realized that leading them was his daughter, now a Wesleyan undergraduate. It was with the opening, however, contrived by Steve Trott, then a Wesleyan Alumni Trustee, that the group definitively staked their claim for primacy. leaving no doubt at all who the real Highwaymen were. An empty stage suddenly came to life as the video image of five young college seniors filled the screen. They were singing "Michael" on the Ed Sullivan Show, and then the curtain went up and there they were—Burnett, Butts, Fisher, and Trott—as if they had never been gone, and the years just slipped away... The original Highwaymen were indeed back.

XI

1987-1991

Got a photograph from a magazine,
gold record hanging from a tambourine;
life was easy, so much fun—
it's a long way down... from Number One.

--The Highwaymen, *In Concert* (2002)
"Number #1" (D. Fisher/A.B. Clyde)

On August 7, 1987, President Ronald Reagan nominated Stephen Trott, then an Associate Attorney General in the Department of Justice, to the United States Court of Appeals for the 9th Circuit, to fill the seat vacated by Joseph Tyree Snead III. The following March, Trott was confirmed by the Senate, receiving his commission the next day. This member of the original Highwaymen was now a Federal judge.

It was now time to address the issue of who were the real Highwaymen. Burnett, Butts, Fisher, and Trott had always considered the name "active, alive, and theirs". Dave Fisher attended a 1989 concert by the new country & western supergroup calling themselves "The Highwaymen", and he took careful note of that quartet's successful merchandising of the Highwaymen name. Thus it happened that the original Highwaymen filed a lawsuit against

145

Johnny Cash, Waylon Jennings, Kris Kristofferson, and Willie Nelson. Certainly there had been "other" Highwaymen before. Gil Robbins, Renny Temple, and Moses MacNaughten were still involved in the music industry, and they would now and then refer to their "Highwaymen" pasts. But this was something different.

The two lawyers in the group—Bob Burnett and Steve Trott—were somewhat surprised by the reaction of the supergroup's attorneys, who seemed determined to contest the suit. Trott was obligated to reveal his status as a Federal judge, but the upstart Highwaymen (or at least their legal counsel) remained unimpressed.

Highwaymen v. Highwaymen began to slowly wend its way through the legal system, but both Waylon Jennings and Judge Trott felt that an amicable settlement would be better for all involved. According to his 9th Circuit colleague, Judge Alex Kozinski, Steve Trott got on the phone with Waylon Jennings, and together they brokered an arrangement which would satisfy all parties. Jennings and his partners agreed that Trott and his colleagues owned their name—the Highwaymen. This original group, in turn, gave the newer "Highwaymen" nonexclusive, nontransferable license to use the name, so that they could continue to tour and record. The original Highwaymen could, of course, use the name as well. To seal the deal, they committed to doing a concert together.

Before that could happen, Johnny Cash came to Boise, Idaho, to perform at the Ada County Fair, doing two shows a night. Steve and Carol Trott attended the first show, and after the performance Steve handed his judicial business card to the stage manager, asking him to pass it on to the Man in Black. "To my surprise," recalled Trott,

Johnny immediately invited Carol and me to join him in

his luxury touring bus where he and June were relaxing between performances. At first, all Johnny could do was apologize for using our name without permission. He said he was well aware of the Highwaymen, having worked with us in the 60s, but that the lawyers told them not to worry, that we were no longer active. I told him not to fret about the past, that we were focused on the future and delighted with the settlement of the lawsuit. The prospect of a joint concert featuring both groups was quite exciting. We then spent time talking about our groups, our music, and especially how much Johnny loved playing county fairs. All of a sudden he said, "I have a great idea! Why don't you come onstage with us during our second show?"

Trott was surprised by the offer. "On the one hand," he thought, it was "a dream come true" to sing with Johnny Cash. On the other hand "it threatened to be a total disaster." Trott replied that they hadn't rehearsed and it might not be a good idea. But Cash said "Well, it's show time. I'm calling you up right after the Carter sisters do their bit. Are you ready?" Trott paused for a moment, gulped, and said, "Johnny, if you're crazy enough to call me up, I'm crazy enough to come."

As the second show began, Steve and Carol Trott made their way back to their seats. Along the way, they encountered two of Steve's law clerks, who wondered what Judge Trott was doing there. Casually, he answered that he was "just going to sing a couple of songs with Johnny." They stared at him in disbelief. The show went on. The Carter Sisters performed. Then Johnny Cash approached the microphone at center stage. "How many of you folks remember the Highwaymen from the 1960s?" he asked the audience. "You know, 'Michael Row the Boat Ashore'?" There was scattered applause.

"Well," Johnny continued,

...me and some friends—Waylon Jennings, Kris Kristofferson

and Willie Nelson—get together sometimes and, with the kind
permission of the original Highwaymen, we use their name…
One of those original Highwaymen, Steve Trott, lives right
here in Boise, and he's here tonight. Let's bring him up and
we'll sing some songs together.

There was more applause as Trott came up on to the stage. Johnny
handed over his guitar, and they sang "Michael" together, "flanked by
June and backed up by his fabulous band," recalled the judge some
years later. "Then we thundered through 'Cotton Fields', complete
with country drums and piano. What a blast!" When Steve Trott tried
to make his exit after the song was done, June Carter put her arm
around him and asked where he thought he was going. Steve Trott
stayed on stage for the concert's last few songs, about fifteen or
twenty minutes up on stage singing with Johnny and June Carter Cash.
The show ended to loud cheers and tumultuous applause. June hugged
their guest and Johnny shook his hand, saying "see you at Universal."

It was just a short while later, on October 1, 1990, at Los Angeles'
Universal Amphitheater, that the first and only Highwaymen concert
co-starring the Highwaymen took place. The two groups, old and new,
folk and country, shared the stage. The original Highwaymen were
greeted "warmly and enthusiastically", recalled one participant, and
they received two standing ovations. "It was very well done,"
remembered Ken Greengrass. In the audience was a colleague of
Steve Trott's on the U.S. Ninth Circuit Court of Appeals—Judge
Robert M. Takasugi—who would have presided over the *Highwaymen
v. Highwaymen* lawsuit if it had come to trial. Backstage, Steve Trott
approached Willie Nelson. "Hey, Willie," he asked, "What's the
matter with you? You were around in the sixties. We were around in
the sixties. How come you stole our name?" Nelson, reported Trott,

just looked at him for a moment, and then answered: "If you can remember the sixties, you must not have been there." A funny line (Wavy Gravy may have said it first), but more significant because of its subtext: the Highwaymen were from that part of the early sixties that didn't last past 1965 (some would say it began to end that November day in Dallas, some two years before). The atmosphere which gave rise to a clean-cut collegiate folk group with a polished style and an honest passion for authenticity as well as commercial aspirations would soon give way to the turmoil of the decade's second half. It was those later sixties, after the Highwaymen had grown up and moved on to other things, to which Nelson was referring.

Buoyed by their Los Angeles reception, the four Highwaymen began to give more performances in the early 1990s. In January of 1991, they were on stage at the 6th Annual WFMA Benefit Concert. It was their first appearance at that increasingly significant event, and it was all the more challenging because Dave Fisher was suffering from laryngitis. Still, they were welcomed enthusiastically. Also on the WFMA stage that January were other great folk performers. Schooner Fare was there. Gibson and Camp were reunited for a powerful set. The creative pair of singer-songwriters David Buskin and Robin Batteau performed. These former sidemen for Tom Rush had been collaborating since the 1980s, when their biggest hit was a Chevrolet commercial ("Listen to the heartbeat, of America")—shades of the Limeliters and the Hillside Singers. That year at the Benefit Concert, Robin Batteau received the WFMA's Kate Wolf Award. Previous recipients had been Utah Phillips, Rosalie Sorrels, and the irrepressibly irreverent Christine Lavin. Perhaps the most anticipated and affecting reunion of the evening was that of original Kingston Trio members Nick Reynolds (who had rejoined Bob Shane as part of the

Trio in the late '80s) and Dave Guard. Less than two months later, Dave Guard was dead, and the fathers of the folk revival had lost an irreplaceable piece of themselves.

Later that summer, the four original Highwaymen performed concerts in venues as far apart as Hawaii and Mystic, Connecticut. They were enjoying their opportunities to play and sing together when they could find the time amidst their busy schedules. Steve Butts was now Director of Evaluation and Planning at Iowa's Grinnell College. Bob and Cathy Burnett were living in Barrington, Rhode Island where he was Senior Vice President of the Rhode Island Trust Bank. Steve Trott still travelled the 9th Circuit, and he and his wife Carol made their home in Boise, Idaho. Dave Fisher was still in Los Angeles, composing and arranging music for television and films. During the mid-80s, he had been involved with the earliest HBO TV series, *1st & Ten*. Fisher continued to work on other shows and films, not only as a composer but also as a music editor and supervisor, often alongside friends and colleagues A.B. Clyde and Byron M. "Rocky" Davis. With all this going on in their far flung lives, a couple of shows a year was all the original Highwaymen could manage.

*   *   *   *   *   *   *   *

Through all this time, other Highwaymen had been busy as well. Gil Robbins was making a name for himself as a composer and conductor of contemporary choral music in New York City, even as he watched his son, Tim, climb the ladder of acting stardom with films like *Bull Durham* and *The Player*. The elder Robbins had served as musical consultant for National Geographic's *American Adventure* series, and he scored a triumph as choral conductor for *Missa*

Gaia/Earth Mass with the Paul Winter Consort at New York's Cathedral of St. John the Divine. Also still involved in music was Moses MacNaughten—the Mose Henry of the Highwaymen's brief '65-'66 incarnation. After surviving a terrible automobile accident, MacNaughten started working—like David Fisher—in films and television. He worked with Manfred Mann on *Christa*, the first feature film completely edited to the beat of the music, where he used a newly arranged version of his "Never a Thought for Tomorrow" from his first Highwaymen album. He would also collaborate with famed director John Avildsen on a number of projects. MacNaughten composed new music for the 23rd Psalm, and his version was selected for the soundtrack of the film used at Abraham Lincoln's birthplace in Hodgenville, Kentucky. Over the years, the former Mose Henry would become increasingly involved in religious, spiritual, and environmental causes. His old friend and fellow bandmate Renny Temple had begun a new career as early as the mid-1980s. After several years as an actor, Temple started directing television sit-coms like *Growing Pains* and *Empty Nest*. The Highwaymen experience, it seems, had been a cradle of and even a crucible for an assortment of creative talent.

In 1991, EMI, which owned the rights to many classic recordings—including everything from old United Artists label-- launched their *Legends of Rock n' Roll* series. "Michael" began appearing on compilation CDs with names like *The Greatest Hits of Rock n' Roll*, and EMI came out with a series of collector's cards. The front side of card #24 featured a photo of five fresh-scrubbed college boys, smiling at the camera, resplendent in their matching vests. Steve Butts sits front and center, holding a banjo. He is flanked on his right by David Fisher, cradling his guitar, and on the left by Steve Trott, leaning on a drum. Behind them, Bob Burnett holds a pair of maracas, while Chan Daniels too sports a guitar. On the reverse side of the card was a brief bio of the group and facts about their two biggest hits: "Michael" and "Cotton Fields". Despite the irony of their being ranked among the *EMI Legends of Rock n' Roll* (Dave Fisher was a long way from the Academics and the Highwaymen had traveled many miles since that first fraternity house show), it was all very gratifying. EMI followed this up with the 1992 release of *Michael Row The Boat Ashore: the best of the Highwaymen*, a CD from its *Legendary Masters* series. Twenty-four Highwaymen songs were featured on the disc, at least one from each of their eight albums (1961-1964), along with the lost single, "All My Trials" (1963), and 1974's "Number #1". The liner notes, by Dave Fisher and Steve Kolanjian, were incredibly detailed, as was Kolanjian's thorough discography. The 1965-1966 Highwaymen, their four 45 releases and their two ABC-Paramount LPs—*On A New Road* and *Stop! Look! & Listen!* — were all included, thereby asserting the continuation of the Highwaymen franchise beyond the disbanding of the original group.

It was an impressive compilation, calling attention to a variety of Highwaymen material (although there were no songs in other languages on the CD). While the big hits and all of the group's charted singles were included, there were also a number of gems which hadn't been heard for many years. Indeed, most of the people who bought the CD were listening to "Number #1" for the very first time.

With EMI's release of their greatest hits CD, the Highwaymen decided to return to the recording studio, creating fresh "product" to be sold at their occasional concerts. This effort, it was felt, would also strengthen their claim to the ownership of the group's name. David Fisher had done a great deal of work for Universal Pictures, and they loaned him use of a Los Angeles studio. The four original Highwaymen then laid down a number of tracks, including "Michael" (but not "Cotton Fields"), "The Gypsy Rover", "I Know Where I'm Going", and "Whisky in the Jar". Another old Highwaymen song, "Work of the Weavers" was artfully rewritten before recording. "La Bamba" was their foreign language song, Steve Trott taking the Spanish lead that Chan Daniels had sung on the *One More Time* LP. A real treat was the Highwaymen's cover of Huddie Ledbetter's "Goodnight Irene", best known from the Weavers' chart-topping version in 1950. Fisher, Burnett, Butts, and Trott each took a verse, and on the chorus all four recaptured the sound of that "fifth member" quite beautifully.

There were three self-referential songs that emerged from those Los Angeles sessions. The take of "Number #1" sounded very much like the 1974 single, with a similar backing track and echoes of Chan Daniels' voice. "The Glory Years", originally written by Fisher, A.B. Clyde, and Rocky Davis for a TV-movie of the same name, had been reworked with the Highwaymen in mind. Looking wistfully back to the past while expressing genuine hope for the future, it was nicely done with Fisher singing the lead. In many ways, the most effective and affecting of the three was a David Fisher/A.B. Clyde collaboration, "When the Village Was Green". Originally inspired by an *Atlantic Monthly* article about Greenwich Village at the height of the folk revival, it opens with a lovely solo line by Steve Butts. Dave Fisher takes his turn, and the two then come together in a duet, while the "fifth member" sings the closing line "...when the Village was green." The layered detail of its description—"a cup of black coffee, a cold café window, I'm watching the rain turn to snow"—gives the song a depth of feeling that is quite powerful. Although some thirty years after the pinnacle of their collective career, it was clear that the Highwaymen hadn't lost it.

* * * * * * * *

Neither, it seems, had other folksingers in the 1990s lost their touch. The Limeliters continued to do very well in concert. After Red Grammer left the trio in 1991 to pursue a music career as a children's artist, Lou Gottlieb and Alex Hassilev added Rick Dougherty to the group, and the Limeliters didn't skip a beat. The Brothers Four, while also experiencing lineup changes, played concerts throughout the world, achieving particular success with Japanese fans. These old combinations vied with newer groups like Four Bitchin' Babes (Christine Lavin, Julie Gold, Sally Fingerett, and Megan McDonough), Side by Side (Doris Justice and Sean McGhee), and the husband-and-wife team of Steve Gillette and Cindy Mangsen for a share of the folk audience. Schooner Fare remained an extremely popular mainstay of the annual World Folk Music Association Benefit concerts. The WFMA also continued to honor folk music's best. The remarkable Odetta received the very first WFMA Lifetime Achievement Award, while the uniquely effervescent Dr. Lou Gottlieb of the Limeliters was its second recipient. Among those who won the WFMA's Kate Wolf Award in the early '90s were Crow Johnson, Hugh Romney (Wavy Gravy), and Peter Yarrow of Peter, Paul, & Mary. This last combo remained most prominent among folk groups in the public eye. A series of annual PBS specials and an abbreviated tour of concert dates endeared them to a new generation, while in 1990 they released their *Flowers & Stones* album, singing songs by Tom Paxton, Bob Dylan, and Pete Seeger. After thirty years, Peter, Paul, & Mary were the most successful folk group ever in the history of the Billboard charts, with eight gold (five of them platinum) albums to their credit and 19 individual songs charted in Billboard's Hot 100. Only the Kingston Trio and Limeliters came anywhere near in album sales. Only the Kingston Trio's and the Highwaymen's output of charted singles came anywhere close. Only the Kingston Trio, Brothers Four, and Limeliters ever approached PP&M's Grammy success among folk groups originating during "The Great Folk Music Scare".

During this time, another folk-indebted performer emerged, like the original Highwaymen, from Wesleyan University. Dar Williams, a singer-songwriter of self-defined "folk-pop", opened for Joan Baez before becoming a successful recording and performing artist in her own right. While the singer-songwriters of the 80s and 90s were the direct descendants of the 60s folk revival, music from that earlier period was once again popular. *The Time-Life Treasury of Folk Music* (four cassettes or CDs) sold very well (and the Highwaymen and the Kingston Trio had more songs in that collection than any other folk groups). There were several re-releases of 60s folk albums on CD, including recordings by the Brothers Four, the Limeliters, the Journeymen, the Kingston Trio, the Brandywine Singers, the New Christy Minstrels, and the Gil Robbins/John Stewart Cumberland Three. Dave Fisher was involved in getting the Cumberland Three's *Songs of the Civil War* out on CD. Businesses like Collector's Choice Music, Rediscover Music, and FolkEra Records made it simpler to find old recordings, while the new CD technology made it easier to re-release them. It was, indeed, a fun time for folk musicians old and new. Highwaymen had come and gone over the years, but the four surviving original members remained a significant part of the folk scene, and they had even added a new Highwayman to the act.

XII

1991-2001

Sing with me, I'll sing with you
and so we will sing together
as we march along.

--The Highwaymen, *March On Brothers!* (1963)
"Marching to Pretoria" (G. Rubin/D. Fisher)

Ever since that Mexican garbageman had taught him how to play, Steve Trott had always loved the guitar. In Boise, he had helped found the Idaho Classical Guitar Society, and in the early 1990s, he met the man who would, for all intents and purposes, become the newest member of the Highwaymen family.

Johann Helton was playing his classical guitar at a local Boise venue when a tall man in his fifties walked on to the patio. "He's playing a Ramirez!" Helton heard Judge Trott exclaim to his wife. Steve and Carol Trott seated themselves at the table closest to the guitarist, "about five feet away," Helton remembered. The couple, he noted, then "proceeded to give me their undivided attention." As Helton continued playing, the stranger studied his fingering and fret work carefully, as if it were the only thing in the world. "He must've thought I was crazy," said Trott later.

"I was not comfortable," admitted Helton,

…but they were very gracious. Anytime I'd play something
Steve didn't recognize, he'd ask me about it. Most of the time
it was an original piece. By the end of the evening, Steve asked
about lessons, and I gave him my card. That week he gave me
a call, and he began coming over to my house on a weekly
basis…

One day, upon arriving at Helton's home, Trott noticed a double bass in the living room. "I didn't know you played one of those," he commented to his host. Helton admitted that he "sort of, kind of" did. It had been his secondary instrument in college, and he had begun his musical career in junior high playing electric bass in a rock n' roll band. Trott's eyes began to twinkle. "I asked him," the judge would later recall, "if he was interested in learning forty or more folk songs and going out on the road with us as our bassist. I didn't say anything about any money." He forgot to mention the group's name as well, and when Helton learned that they were the Highwaymen, so prominent among his boyhood recollections, he was thrilled. "A few months later," Helton remembered, "the Highwaymen came to Idaho to perform, and I became their bass player." Thus a partnership was formed.

Helton, an experienced musician both as performer and composer, was a terrific addition to the group. *The Boise Weekly* described him as "…one of Idaho's best loved guitarists." The Highwaymen would introduce him to audiences as "our good friend from Boise, Idaho." He would provide a strong rhythm background for the four folk performers and lent a greater depth and substance to their sound.

*   *   *   *   *   *   *   *

A very special folk reunion took place in 1993. New York City's 92nd Street Y was the scene of a concert which featured Pete Seeger, Oscar Brand, Burl Ives, Theodore Bikel, Tom Paxton, and the Chad Mitchell Trio. It was an event powerful in its nostalgia, and it resonated emotionally with its audience. Between them, the performers had more almost 300 years of folksinging experience. It was also Burl Ives' last time in the spotlight. At least he had been able, at the last, to share a stage with Pete Seeger—the man who named names and the man who refused to name names, finally together again. Burl Ives passed away in 1995.

In 1996, the folk music world was saddened by the death of the Limeliters' Lou Gottlieb. Only a short while before, the group had performed at a Chad Mitchell Trio reunion concert alongside Carolyn Hester and Christine Lavin. Former Limeliter Glenn Yarborough sang at his old friend's funeral. Gottlieb's high baritone part for the Limeliters was soon taken up by Bill Zorn, formerly of the Kingston Trio and the New Christy Minstrels. The music would go on.

With Johann Helton and his bass along, the original Highwaymen traveled to Washington, DC for their second scheduled appearance at a World Folk Music Association Benefit. Shortly before that event, the group attended a Schooner Fare concert, and the Highwaymen joined that talented trio onstage to sing. Then came the 11th Annual WFMA Benefit Concert. Also performing there, along with the Highwaymen, were Side by Side, Eddie from Ohio, Bill Danoff, Pete and Maura Kennedy, Chesapeake, Catie Curtis, Dee Carstensen, and the witty folk satire of the Foremen. After thanking Dick Cerri and his staff for their kindness and hospitality, Dave Fisher told the audience that they would be "singing the songs our fathers sang so long ago." The Highwaymen opened the second half of the show with classic renditions of "Gypsy Rover" and the "Irish Work Song", and then delighted the packed house with their medley of "Michael" and "Number #1".

It was a special night for folk music, as Oscar Brand, the godfather of the folk revival, was honored with the WFMA Lifetime Achievement Award. The great Jean Ritchie, Brand's longtime friend and collaborator, presented him with the award, and the audience gave them a standing ovation. Later, after Carolyn Hester presented Nancy Griffith with the Kate Wolf Award, and after Schooner Fare closed out the evening with a well-received set mixing soft ballads with robust crowd-pleasers, all the performers gathered on stage to sing together a rousing rendition of "The Midnight Special". The Highwaymen were in their element.

The original four weren't the only Highwaymen to shine throughout the 1990s. Tim Robbins' motion picture career had reached out to involve his father. Gil Robbins was cast in four films during the decade. In his son's 1992 picture *Bob Roberts* he played Reverend Best. Two more clergy roles—as Bishop Norwich in *Dead Man Walking* (1995) and Cardinal Geary in M. Night Shyamalan's *Wide Awake* (1998)—followed. Moving from heaven to hell, Gil Robbins shed his clerical collar to play Congressman Starnes in Tim Robbins' 1999 drama *Cradle Will Rock*. Through all this time, he never was far from his music. He did choral arrangements and conducted for the soundtrack of son Tim's *Dead Man Walking*, and he also arranged choral music for the film *Savior* (1998) for which his son David wrote the score. Moses MacNaughten, meanwhile, was becoming increasingly active as a performer, appearing at an Earth Day concert in 1996 and at environmental events across the country.

He also was instrumental in founding One Heart Global Broadcasting with his wife, artist Lisa Lloyd, whose "One Heart" poster for the U.N. was used on PBS and received an award from the Earth Society Foundation.

There were awards aplenty for folk performers as the new millennium dawned. The 2000 Kate Wolf Award went to Noel Paul Stookey, the former folk comedian and MC at the Gaslight Café who had gone on to phenomenal success as one-third of Peter, Paul, & Mary. He was following in the footsteps of recent recipients Jack Hardy, Tom Chapin, David Buskin, and Nina Gerber, as well as those of his longtime partner and collaborator Peter Yarrow. The 1997 and 1998 WFMA Lifetime Achievement Awards were, sadly, both posthumously presented. The late Bob Gibson was the recipient in 1997, while John Denver—whose death in a flying accident had shocked the world—was honored the following year. Tom Paxton made both presentations. In 1999, the recipient was also not able to accept the WFMA's Lifetime Achievement Award, but only because a massive snowstorm prevented Tommy Makem from being on hand. The following month, he received the award in Gaithersburg, Maryland, appropriately enough at Mrs. O'Leary's Pub. In 2000, the founder of the Kerrville Folk Festival, Rod Kennedy, was recognized by the WFMA for Lifetime Achievement. This well-deserved honor was particularly satisfying to Carolyn Hester, who had served on the Festival's Board for many years. In January of the following year, former Cumberland Three and Kingston Trio member John Stewart received the award. Gil Robbins' old music student had come a long way from those early days at Pomona Catholic High School.

In 1998, the World Folk Music Association established a new award in memory of John Denver. It was first presented in January of

1999 to Milt Okun, John Denver's original publisher and producer; the man who helped bring together Peter, Paul & Mary and who produced the Highwaymen's *March On Brothers!* LP. John Denver's good friend Kenn Roberts, a member of the Washington, DC folk group the Hard Travelers and the producer of the *Tribute to John Denver* concert series received the award in 2000, while Denver's old partner Bill Danoff, producer of *John Denver Remembered—by the old Cellar Door Gang*, was the recipient in January 2001.

Folk music, then, was seeing fit to recognize its past, even as it encouraged new creations. In 1999, the Limeliters released a new studio album. The CD was called *Until We Get It Right*, and the title song was hilariously and wonderfully sung by Rick Dougherty. That same year, Bob Gibson's old partner Hamilton (nee Bob) Camp released a new solo album, *Mardi's Bard*. Schooner Fare was also among those groups continuing to come out with new recordings throughout the '90s and into the new century. So were the Highwaymen. Their newest CD, from those recording sessions earlier in the decade, was called *Still Rowing*. Although the music was lovely, it had all the earmarks of a homemade release ("I think Fisher put that together in his bathtub," joked Steve Butts), but at least Universal had been generous with its studio time and its support. It did give the group something to have for their fans at their occasional concert appearances, and it kept the Highwaymen name alive.

*　*　*　*　*　*　*　*

In the summer of 2000, the Highwaymen performed at a benefit concert for the Clearview School of the Association for Mentally Ill Children in Briarcliff Manor, New York. Clearview's Medical

Director, Dr. Elaine Haagen, appeared on stage with her husband, Dave Fisher, and they sang "The Great Silkie" as a lovely duet, accompanied by Steve Butts on the baroque oboe d'amore. Despite rough weather outside, the audience was enthusiastic, and the show was energetic and full of life. In addition to their old favorites—there was vigorous applause after just the first few notes of Butts' whistling intro to "Michael"—there was new material as well. Tommy Makem's "Red is the Rose" invited audience participation, while two numbers by New England singer-songwriter Bill Staines (the oft-covered "Place in the Choir" and that New Hampshire balladeer's signature song, "River") went over well. There was also a country-folk collaboration, as David Fisher combined Johnny Cash's take on "Streets of Laredo" with a more traditional version, to great effect. There were certainly no hard feelings about those "other" Highwaymen. Fisher credited their "good friend Johnny Cash," and continued "...who, by the way, is doing well... singing again and everything." The group's tribute to Chan Daniels, "Carnivalito", was performed with exuberant zest, and even their occasional mistakes were absorbed into the general good humor of the evening.

By this time, the Highwaymen were recording all of their concerts, hoping at some point to produce a high-quality CD of live performances. There was plenty of time, however. Steve Trott continued to preside as a Federal judge on the 9th Circuit. He would make fun of this in concert—"You're all under arrest!" he would tell the audience—but he'd also creatively bend and twist the story of their lawsuit with those "other" Highwaymen to put himself comically at the center: "...and when they saw who was on the bench, they caved in—gives a whole new meaning to the phrase 'home court advantage', don't you think?" In addition to his

Norman Blake model Martin guitar, Trott was now also playing a Phoenix mandolin (by the legendary Rolfe Gerhardt) with the group. Bob Burnett was now a Vice President at Fleet Bank in Rhode Island, and in his spare moments the old Wesleyan track letterman would run in local races, including several marathons. Steve Butts was by this time Director of Institutional Research at Lawrence University in Appleton, Wisconsin where he also lectured in music and served as co-Director of Lawrence's Collegium Musicum. In addition to his Gibson Mastertone flattop banjo with a custom neck by John D'Angelico, he was also playing the baroque oboe, involved in master classes at Oberlin College and teaching baroque music at the Lawrence Conservatory. Dave Fisher was dividing his life between Los Angeles and Rye, and he was finding more and more opportunities to create new arrangements for the Highwaymen. They loved to sing together and enjoyed their chances to perform onstage when their busy calendars allowed. 2000 slipped into 2001, and the Highwaymen maintained their schedule of a handful of concerts each year. They celebrated with Johann Helton that spring when he released his first solo album, *Where Mountains End and Clouds Begin*. An instrumental collection of original compositions for nylon-string guitar, it was favorably reviewed by the *Idaho Statesman*, as

> a polished, soothing...collection of relaxed musical
> moods - somber, romantic, yearning, dreamy.

It wouldn't last. The relaxed mood of an entire nation was shattered just a few months later, by the events of September 11, 2001.

The earliest "official" photograph of The Highwaymen, taken in 1960, on the campus of Wesleyan University.

from the collection of the author

Both the group's debut LP and their first 45 charted: "Michael", the B-side of their single climbed the charts to number one. Over the years, "Michael" has sold more than five million records and has been played on the air yet another five million times: perhaps the most successful traditional folk song recording ever made!

While maintaining their busy academic, athletic, and social schedules, the five Highwaymen found time to rehearse, to select and arrange new songs, and to sing around the Wesleyan campus.

photos from the author's collection

"Cotton Fields" became the group's second big hit single, remaining in the Top 40 for more than three months. Their second LP, "Standing Room Only!", also charted.

"Encore" was the last album by the original five Highwaymen, as they graduated from Wesleyan in 1962.

from the collection of the author

The Highwaymen were among the leaders in sheet music and songbook sales worldwide.

from the author's collection

They were also among the top-selling groups internationally.
According to one British poll, they were the second most popular
group in the world for 1961-62, behind the Everly Brothers.

By the autumn of 1962, the Highwaymen were a quartet, Gil Robbins joining them on their next album, "March On, Brothers".

Steve Butts

Chan Daniels

Gil Robbins

Dave Fisher

The Highwaymen

from the collection of the author

With the return of Bob Burnett in the spring of 1963, there were once again five Highwaymen, and based in Greenwich Village, they recorded their next LP. The live "Hootenanny with the Highwaymen" made the Billboard charts: their most successful album since "Standing Room Only!".

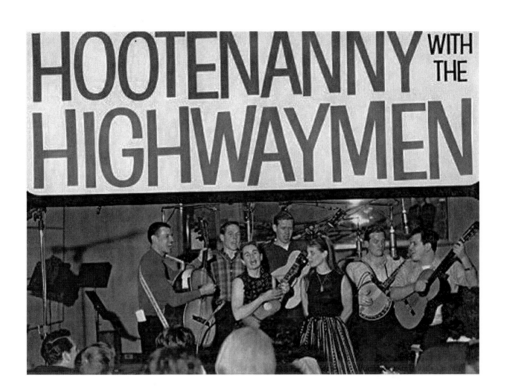

from the collection of the author

The group's next album, produced by Fred Hellerman, "One More Time!" features some of their finest work.

*"One More Time!" also introduced The Highwaymen logo,
designed by Gerry Olin Greengrass. Only two years later, with the
Highwaymen disbanded, it would be copied by The Monkees.*

from the author's collection

In February of 1964, The Highwaymen returned to the campus of Wesleyan University to record their next album live.

"Homecoming!" was indeed just that, culled from two concerts in the Wesleyan Chapel.

The Highwaymen back on campus, not far from where they posed for their first "official" photos as fledgling recording artists.

The Highwaymen at their last Ed Sullivan appearance, on August 16, 1964; from left to right: Daniels, Burnett, Robbins (playing the guitarron), Fisher, and Butts.

photo by Ed Sullivan Productions, from www.originalhighwaymen.com

from the author's collection

The final Highwaymen LP, released in October of 1964. By then, the group had broken up. After almost five years, with three albums and ten singles on the charts, including two Top 40 hits and perhaps the most successful folk recording of all time, The Highwaymen had called it quits.

from the author's collection

Over the next quarter century, two other groups would call themselves The Highwaymen. The first, pictured above, was put together by Ken Greengrass and David Fisher, and lasted only from 1965-1966. The second, of course, was the Country-and-Western supergroup of Johnny Cash, Waylon Jennings, Kris Kristofferson and Willie Nelson. They first got together in the late 1980s. In 1990, a lawsuit filed by the original Highwaymen against this new quartet was settled amicably, and the two legendary groups performed a concert together.

In 1990, EMI issued a series of collector's cards as part of its Legends of Rock n' Roll series. The Highwaymen were featured on card #24, and a compilation of their greatest hits was also released for EMI's Legendary Masters series.

Steve Trott and Dave Fisher relaxing on the deck of Bob Burnett's Rhode Island home in the early 1990s.

photo by Steve Butts, from www.originalhighwaymen.com

Bob Burnett running in the 1998 New York City Marathon.

photo by Al Burnett,
from www.originalhighwaymen.com

David Fisher, working at the piano.

photo by Charles DePuy, from www.originalhighwaymen.com

Steve Butts, shown here at an Oberlin College master class, warming up with a copy of a Stanesby 3-keyed oboe.

photo by Barbara Trautwein,
from www.originalhighwaymen.com

Steve Trott, telling a story onstage.

photo by Mark Swirsky, from www.originalhighwaymen.com

Johann Helton, classical guitarist.

courtesy Jo-Town Records, from www.originalhighwaymen.com

Ken Greengrass

Don Costa

Over the past decade, the original Highwaymen
have released four new CDs.

The Highwaymen at the 20th Annual World Folk Music Association
Benefit Concert in January of 2005.

photo by Chuck Morse, from http://wfma.net

The Highwaymen today, at the Guthrie Center in western Massachusetts; from left to right: Helton, Fisher, Trott, Butts, and Burnett.

photo by Mark Swirsky, www.familyventures.com from www.originalhighwaymen.com

XIII

2001-2006

River is deep, the river is wide,
milk and honey on the other side…

--The Highwaymen, *The Highwaymen* (1961)
"Michael" (trad/D. Fisher)

Folk musicians, like all Americans, responded to the tragedy of 9/11. "As I watched the events of September 11 like everyone else," Tom Paxton recalled,

> writing a song about it didn't occur to me for hours. When it did, my instinctive reaction was, 'No way. This is over my head. This is too overwhelming for me.' …And then, as I kept thinking about those firemen trapped inside the towers, a phrase kept running through my head. Finally, I surrendered and thought I'd better try to write something … Now, I'll never be able to look at another fireman or-woman without realizing that I'm looking at someone who would lay down his or her life for me without ever knowing my name...

Paxton's song, "The Bravest", would serve as a tribute to the heroes of 9/11, with its haunting chorus:

> Now every time I try to sleep, I'm haunted by the sound
> of firemen pounding up the stairs, while we were running down.

199

It would be covered by a variety of artists from Pete Seeger to Liz McNicholl. It was McNicholl's version which was featured on a special broadcast of *Profiles in Folk*, a regular program on WSHU radio (the National Public Radio station at Connecticut's Sacred Heart University), hosted by Steve Winters. On Friday, November 23, 2001, only a day after Thanksgiving and less than two months after 9/11, Winters featured

> a vehicle for exploring universal themes such as thanks, love, grace, homecoming and justice. This year the show takes on extra meaning because of the Sept. 11 terrorist attacks on America that have established a new spirit and civility across the land and a coming together of the nation.

For that evening's program, Winters selected twenty-one songs, several from among the "many unsolicited releases, mostly CD singles that feature musical responses to those tragic events." The proceeds from almost every one of these songs were intended for 9-11 charities.

In May of 2002, more than two dozen folk musicians traveled to Pittsburgh's Carnegie-Mellon University to participate in the creation of a new Public Television special: *This Land is Your Land—the Folk Years*. Judy Collins and the Smothers Brothers hosted the program, which was taped over two evenings. Bob Shane's latest incarnation of the Kingston Trio (with George Grove and Bob Haworth) was there, along with the current Limeliters (Hassilev, Dougherty, Zorn), who were joined onstage by old friend Glenn Yarborough. The show's hosts performed, of course, along with the Brothers Four, and Barry McGuire sang his classic "Eve of

Destruction". Roger McGuinn sang songs from the Byrds' hit list (with backup vocals from Mike Settle). The original Highwaymen were there, performing "Michael", "Cotton Fields", and "Number #1". Ken Greengrass was proud of the fact that "his boys" received a standing ovation.

The final group to perform was Randy Sparks and the Minstrels, a reincarnation of Sparks' New Christy Minstrels with many of the veteran members returned, including Barry McGuire and Clarence Treat. They sang their old hit, "Green, Green", with McGuire taking the lead. Then they started singing "This Land Is Your Land", but after one chorus they stopped, and Randy Sparks introduced a new song he had written in response to 9-11. The chorus of "Just Americans", a timely plea for tolerance and teamwork, seemed to resonate with the audience.

> On September the eleventh
> we became Just Americans,
> other names were rendered obsolete.
> All I know about my neighbors
> is that they are Just Americans;
> shoulder to shoulder, now, the circle is complete.

Immediately after the applause for "Just Americans" died down, Sparks and his team re-launched Woody Guthrie's "This Land is Your Land", and they were joined on stage by all the show's performers, singing that classic modern folk song shoulder to shoulder and voice to voice.

Just a few days later, the Highwaymen found themselves back at Wesleyan University, to put on a concert for the 40th Reunion of the Class of 1962. This performance featured a new song for the group, "Sailing to Philadelphia", which told the story of the creation of the

Mason-Dixon Line, through the voices of historical figures Jeremiah Dixon and Charles Mason. It was written by Mark Knopfler of Dire Straits, and once again the Highwaymen demonstrated their commitment to develop and grow as musicians and performers. Another song, although a longtime part of the Highwaymen repertoire, allowed the group to invoke the memory of 9-11.

> On October 31, 1941, the United States destroyer, Reuben James, was attacked, torpedoed and sunk while sailing west of Iceland. Ninety-five lives were lost in this, the first U.S. warship to go down in World War II.

With this introduction, Steve Butts began the Highwaymen's rendition of Woody Guthrie's classic song, *The Sinking of the Reuben James*, telling the tale of a shocking incident from the months before Pearl Harbor. This time, however, there was something different about the final verse. They sang

> Many years have past since these brave men are gone, it happened once again on a clear September morn.

The new line, which simply but powerfully connected the past century with the present, would remain for as part of the Highwaymen's repertoire.

*   *   *   *   *   *   *   *

In August of 2002, the Highwaymen returned to their earliest roots when they appeared as the opening act at Milwaukee's annual Irish Fest, hearkening back to their days as the Clansmen. They were the only non-Irish group there, sharing the Miller Stage with artists like Patrick Street, Robbie O'Connell, Liam Clancy, and Cherish the Ladies, just to name a few. Even as Steve Butts was compiling a collection of songs from the group's more recent concerts for a live CD, their focus was on their performance at the Irish Fest, and the Highwaymen were planning a new studio effort, to feature just music from the Celtic tradition.

Their CD *In Concert* was mastered by Johann Helton and Don Cunningham at Cunningham Audio in Boise, Idaho and it became available early in 2003. Like their concerts at the time, the CD opened with perhaps their best recorded rendition of "Number #1". Its humor, with its somewhat updated lyrics, was both timely and delightful, while the immediate audience response was refreshing. Indeed, folk songs and folk performers are almost always better received live than in their studio incarnations, and this CD proved to be no exception. The live version of "Cotton Fields", appearing near the end of the album, might actually be better than the original. At least seven of the songs on this CD had never appeared on any previously released Highwaymen recordings, and at least two others were artfully rewritten and updated. Bill Staines' "Place in the Choir" and "River", Tommy Makem's (actually, Tommy Makem's mother's) "Red is the Rose" adapted and arranged by Steve Butts, and the Fisher/Cash "Streets of Laredo" were all new to the Highwaymen discography.

True to their roots, the group continued to perform in other languages. There were two songs in Spanish on the new CD, both presented as memorial tributes to Chan Daniels. One, "La Bamba", had been recorded before by the Highwaymen. The other, "Guantanamera", had never appeared on a previous release by the group, and Steve Trott provided interesting historical narration, obviously inspired by Pete Seeger's earlier take on the song. One older Highwaymen number, in particular, had an interesting history with the group. "Greenland Fisheries" was recorded for their debut album some four decades earlier, while "Did You Ever See a Wild Goose?" had been part of their live *Homecoming!* LP. On this CD, the two chanties were brought together, using "Wild Goose" as an introduction to the longer whaling song, and then concluding with a coda which had previously been used by the Weavers—in short: three sea chanties blended into one.

Everyone had a chance to shine on the CD. Bob Burnett had arguably his finest Highwaymen moment, taking the lead on Bill Staines' "River". Steve Butts' self-acknowledged "old folkie" turn with Tom Paxton's "Ramblin' Boy" was very effective. Steve Trott guided the listener through much of the group's story, taking the lead on the Spanish numbers. Dave Fisher's soaring tenor was, if anything, richer and more expressive than ever. Finally, the non-musical interludes and introductions proved both hilarious (Steve Trott on the origins of the group and on their confrontation with the "other" Highwaymen) and moving (Steve Butts reflecting on the folk scene in Greenwich Village and how he first encountered Paxton's "Ramblin' Boy").

The *In Concert* CD would be a successful seller at subsequent Highwaymen concerts throughout 2003 and beyond. Also released about the same time was Dave Fisher's first solo effort: a CD entitled *Love's Way*. Dedicated to his wife "Elaine, who makes everything possible", the tender and poignant collection of songs was "about falling in love, losing love, and falling in love all over again." Many of them were co-written by Fisher with his longtime collaborator A.B. Clyde, who also wrote the liner notes. The opening number,

"Angels in my Backyard", had been created some years earlier for a television project, and it beautifully set the mood for a lovely album, which included one traditional folksong—"If I Were a Blackbird". The CD was arranged and produced by David Fisher and his colleague Rocky Davis (who doubled on keyboard for the sessions). *Love's Way* would also be available at Highwaymen concerts.

* * * * * * * *

In early March of 2003, "University of the Air", a regular Sunday afternoon offering on Wisconsin Public Radio, invited Steve Butts to be a guest on the program. The topic was folk music of the sixties, and Butts led his hosts and their listeners through a detailed history and fascinating analysis of the period and its music. Interestingly, many of the song clips he used on the show were taken from a tape he had made of the 1961 WRVR "Folk Music Hootenanny" at Riverside Church, which he had engineered at the same time "Michael" was climbing the charts. Perhaps Butts was anticipating the renewed interest in sixties folk music that would be engendered by the release, later that same month, of the film *A Mighty Wind.*

A self-proclaimed "mockumentary", *A Mighty Wind* could be considered a mock documentary, but not really a mocking one. Indeed, the satire was pointed but fairly gentle, and the whole experience had as much the quality of a tribute as it had of comedy. Director Christopher Guest also co-starred, and his cast parodied such old folk performers as the Kingston Trio, Limeliters, New Christy Minstrels, Serendipity Singers, and Ian & Sylvia, just to name a few. "Significantly," noted Highwayman Steve Butts, "the film parodied only the most 'commercial' groups, while leaving the giants like Pete Seeger, Dylan, *et al,* alone." The original songs were definitely parodies, but they had an authentic sound and were performed so sincerely that there were moments when the audience could be forgiven for thinking that it might just be the real thing. "I loved the movie," Judge Steve Trott said. "Especially at the end, when 'we' (the folksingers) become judges!"

Made with a relatively low production budget, *A Mighty Wind* took in three times its original cost at the box office domestically, and did equally well internationally. Subsequent DVD sales continued its popular success. The film earned a Grammy for its title song, an Academy Award nomination for another number, and, more than anything else, it got people talking about folk music again. Nowhere was this more clearly seen than by the folk performers themselves. Newspapers, magazines, and countless online forums indulged in speculating which of the film's characters or groups was based on what real-life counterpart. And all this did was put the names of folksingers and folk groups back in the public eye. You could find folk concerts everywhere, and folk combos like the Kingston Trio, the Limeliters, and the Shaw Brothers sold out successful "folk cruises" to warmer climes during the winter months.

Dick Cerri and the World Folk Music Association continued to honor those who made lasting contributions to the genre. At the annual WFMA Benefit concerts from 2002-2004, the Kennedys, Ann Hills, and David Massengill had each received the Kate Wolf Memorial Award. Tom Wisner and Magpie had also been named recipients of the John Denver Award. In 2002, the WFMA Lifetime Achievement Award was presented to folksinger and social historian Joe Glazer, author of the classic book *Songs of Work and Protest.* The following year, Carolyn Hester was the recipient of this, the

WFMA's most auspicious honor. Then, on January 16, 2004, Dave Van Ronk was recognized posthumously for his lifetime of achievement to folk music. Van Ronk—Tom Paxton's "gentle giant", the singer who opened each night at the old Gaslight, and the man who was often credited with coining the phrase "Great Folk Music Scare"—had passed away in February of 2002 at the age of 65. Now it was his time to be honored. Less than twenty-four hours after the Van Ronk presentation, however, a stunned WFMA audience learned of the sudden death of Schooner Fare's Tom Rowe, just 54, who had been undergoing cancer treatment. No folk group had been more active and productive over the previous decade than Schooner Fare, and they had appeared at every World Folk Music Benefit concert since its inception. "Tom," said Schooner Fare colleague Chuck Romanoff, "was a man who genuinely loved music, his family and friends, and who enjoyed life and everything it had to offer." Chuck's brother, Steve the third member of the trio, agreed, saying: "Tom embodied the true meaning of the term 'working artist'".

*　*　*　*　*　*　*　*

In 2004, the original Highwaymen released their new Celtic CD, *The Water of Life*. Essentially a studio effort (with just a single live cut), it had been recorded during the summer of 2003 at Johann Helton's JoTown Records in Boise, Idaho. Helton engineered the effort, which was then mastered by Don Cunningham and Dave Fisher at Boise's Cunningham Audio. Contemporary Irish folksinger (and New York University Professor) Mick Moloney, a long-time admirer of the Highwaymen, wrote the introduction to the CD in the liner notes. Moloney, while a visiting lecturer and performer at Wesleyan, had met David Fisher over dinner there. The two had hit it off, even giving an impromptu concert at a local pub in the early hours of the morning. Now the Irish folk scholar was recognizing and honoring the original Highwaymen's latest recording effort (and return to their Clansmen roots). Moloney wrote that he was "delighted" that the original Highwaymen

> are back in the American folk music scene... I hope they get as much enjoyment from the second phase of their performing career as they have given so many of us in the first.

Fourteen songs made the final CD—six Irish, five Scots, one Scots-Irish, and two Irish-American—yet it was the first-ever Highwaymen album released without a song in another language. While over the years the Highwaymen had performed songs in six different languages and from sixteen different countries, *The Water of Life* was, in a way, a return to their earliest musical roots together. The CD opened with Tommy Sands eloquent and more than a little elegiac "Down by the Lagan Side", about Northern Ireland. Bob Burnett sang the lead quite affectingly. The delightfully amusing "Ramblin' Rover", from the contemporary Scottish folksinger Andy Stewart, followed. Steve Butts, Steve Trott, and Bob Burnett each had a verse on the a capella number which segued smoothly into Leo McQuire's modern Irish classic "The Gypsy Rover", highlighted by David Fisher's solo. Fisher, the group's principal arranger, has often liked pairing two different songs, and here it worked seamlessly and effectively.

"Nancy Whisky", that old Scots tune sometimes known as "The Calton Weaver" came next, and Steve Butts delivered it well. The next two numbers were linked as traditional Irish-American songs. "Paddy's Lamentation" had been featured prominently in the film *Gangs of New York*, and on *The Water of Life* CD it became a showcase for Dave Fisher's powerful tenor voice. "Paddy Works on the Railway" was a new recording of the "Irish Work Song" from their very first album. All four of the Highwaymen sang verses on this one.

It was, of course, Tommy Makem who had heard from his mother the old Scots tune "Loch Lomond" sung with Irish lyrics: "Red is the Rose". Steve Butts' arrangement on the CD was very good. Butts also adapted and arranged the only instrumental cut on the album—the "Irish Lamentation Waltz". This tune had its origins, interestingly enough, in Scotland during the time the English were forcing the Scots off their land. It was taken up by the Irish almost a century later when they found themselves facing similar hardships, and in both of these incarnations it was a mournful dirge. Sometime after that, however, the English themselves adopted the melody and with ruthless historical irony transformed it from a lament into a sprightly waltz. It was this latter version the Highwaymen recorded, with Butts demonstrating his skill on the recorder.

The old Highwaymen favorite "Whisky in the Jar" came next on the CD, featuring Dave Fisher's lead solo. Fisher also arranged the old Child Ballad "The Great Silkie" as a duet with his wife, Elaine Haagen. This sad Scottish story was hauntingly and evocatively sung by the two of them, backed by Steve Butts on the oboe d'amore. "Work of the Weavers" then provided a perfect example of David Fisher's "fifth member" of the group. In this reworking of an old Highwaymen favorite, one verse paid homage to those earlier folksinging legends who inspired so much of the modern American folk music scene over the past half century. "Broom of the Cowdenknowes", an older song from the Scots tradition, a version of which had appeared in Francis Child's collection of ballads—and a new song for the Highwaymen—was next.

The CD's final two songs came from Ireland. "Finnegan's Wake" may have first appeared as an English street-ballad mocking the Irish, and in America it represented the negative stereotype of the Irish immigrant as seen on the music hall stage; but somehow the Irish re-adopted it. James Joyce chose the song's comic story as a symbol of a universal life cycle in his book of the same name, and today it is proudly performed as an important part of Irish legacy and heritage, reflecting a genuine Irish historical experience. All that aside, the Highwaymen presented it in a straightforward manner. The group made a wise choice in selecting a live performance of "Finnegan's Wake" from an earlier concert to be their cut of the song on this CD. The audience reaction to the song's comic humor gives the listener the full effect of a delightful experience.

"The Parting Glass" , another traditional Irish song, was adapted by Shaun Davey for the wonderful film *Waking Ned Devine*. The Highwaymen got the song from that picture, and in recent years have used it to end most of their concerts. Dave Fisher's arrangement provided a fitting conclusion to an excellent collection of Celtic folk music.

*   *   *   *   *   *   *   *

Outside of the recording studio, the Highwaymen were enjoying the opportunities they had to play live dates around the country. Some of these were in genuine folk clubs, hearkening back to their earlier days. The Muse at the Grey Goose in Londonderry, New

Hampshire and Arlo Guthrie's Guthrie Center in Great Barrington, Massachusetts were just two of these venues in 2003 and 2004. They performed for private events and in concert at theaters, such as the Blackstone in Cumberland, Rhode Island. Sometimes they would resurrect old favorites such as the lovely Fisher/Butts duet on "Marianne". There was new material as well. "Daughters and Sons", Tommy Sands' passionate and personal plea for peace and justice, allowed the Highwaymen to give their audience a more serious and intense sing-along experience. This intensity remained leavened by the comic reminiscences of skilled performers bringing to the show a wide range of instruments including guitar, banjo, bass, mandolin, recorder, and baroque oboe. With exquisite harmonies, impressive song selection, and an obvious rapport with the audience, it was clear that the Highwaymen continued to take delight in their ongoing musical career.

This delight was most evident at the 20th Annual World Folk Music Association Benefit Weekend where, over two nights in January of 2005, the original Highwaymen joined with much of the folk music world to sing together and to celebrate their common heritage. The Brothers Four were there, with original member Bob Flick leaning on his bass, still smiling as he introduced his newer compatriots. There were the Limeliters—Alex Hassilev with his latest partners Andy Corwin and Mack Bailey. From the old days, there was folk music legend Oscar Brand, who proved that he had not lost his touch by telling stories and singing songs at both the Saturday afternoon workshops and at the show that same evening. Hamilton Camp, Carolyn Hester and David Blume, the original Chad Mitchell Trio, Steve Gillette and Cindy Mangsen, Bill Danoff, Noel Paul Stookey (some forty-five years after his gig as MC at the

Gaslight), and the legendary Tommy Makem were also on hand. Stookey told the audience about the continuing recovery of his longtime friend and colleague Mary Travers from leukemia. Tommy Makem had the crowd on its feet with his powerful rendition of "Four Green Fields", accompanied by his son Rory. Newer acts, at least relatively, were featured as well. Gracing the stage of the Birchmere in Alexandria, Virginia were Side by Side, Buskin & Batteau, and Modern Man. David Mallett was there, as were Chuck and Steve Romanoff of Schooner Fare. The wild and crazy Christine Lavin seemed to be everywhere at once, on both nights and at the workshops on Saturday.

Awards, of course, were presented. The late Tom Rowe of Schooner Fare received the Kate Wolf Memorial Award. The highlight of Friday evening's show was a very special presentation by Tom Paxton. He surprised WFMA co-founder Dick Cerri with the Lifetime Achievement Award, and the audience held up signs of thanks, giving Cerri a standing ovation.

On Saturday evening, the original Highwaymen took to the stage. They opened their set with the a capella Scots number "Ramblin' Rover", written by Andy Stewart, transitioning smoothly into the Irish "Gypsy Rover". Their "Sinking of the Reuben James", with its nod to 9-11, followed. A powerful "Daughters and Sons" sing-along held the attention of the crowd, which then delighted in "Number #1" and burst into loud applause for "Michael". Six songs—three from the group's earliest days at the height of their popularity, and three newer numbers from more recent years—saw the Highwaymen in their element, secure in their place as one of the important bands in modern folk music history.

At the end of both shows, all the performers gathered on stage.

Led by the Limeliters' Alex Hassilev, they sang together with the audience on Ed McCurdy's stirring plea for peace, "Last Night I Had the Strangest Dream". Then everyone followed Side by Side's Sean McGhee, singing

Come on, people now, smile on your brother
everybody get together, try to love one another
right now.

That weekend in January of 2005, the power of folk music—its passion and its permanence—made itself known, and felt.

POSTLUDE

Looking Ahead—through 2008 and beyond...

...and in this never-ending story,
there'll be glory years ahead for us.

--The Highwaymen, *Still Rowing* (1999)
"The Glory Years" (D. Fisher/A.B. Clyde/R. Davis)

2008 – Fifty years ago, when five young men first met on the campus of Wesleyan University, they had no way of knowing that their efforts would still continue to bear fruit a half-century later. The Folk Revival was at its peak, "The Great Folk Music Scare" had exploded on to the popular scene, and soon the Highwaymen were swept up in its wondrous whirlwind of sold-out concerts and million-selling recordings. Their "Michael" was only the third folk song ever to top the charts. Those were indeed "years of glory", unexpected and unprecedented, and the Highwaymen certainly made the most of their opportunities. From gold record hits and television appearances to late-night shows in the dim-lit caverns of Greenwich Village, their adventures carried them into every corner of the folk revival experience. Then they, like so many, parted company, only to reunite again to share among themselves and with others their love and enthusiasm for folk music.

Not long ago, David Fisher re-visited Greenwich Village, once again walking the streets and seeing the places which had been so much a part of his life and the lives of so many others, back when "the Great Folk Music Scare" was in full flower. But Greenwich Village is no longer what it was in the era of the Washington Square folk riot. The Gaslight is gone—indeed, most of the old folk clubs are no longer there. Some remain, like the Bitter End, but the music is different (although in no small way indebted to its folk forebears). Still, there are everywhere echoes of that special time. In 2005, Oscar Brand still hosted his long-running radio show (recorded from Jean Ritchie's Manhattan apartment), while New York remained and still remains a vibrant, creative presence in the lives of new generations of singers and songwriters.

In September of 2007, Sam Hood— "the heart and spirit of the Gaslight Café," according to Highwayman Steve Butts—passed away. "For us," Butts remembered, "he was an enthusiastic guide to both the glory and the netherworld of Village life in that most wonderful of times, and above all, a constant and true friend... Sam was at the center of and a key force in the folk renaissance that flowered in Greenwich Village, New York."

New York remains home to Ken Greengrass, perhaps the oldest member of the Highwaymen "family". From his eastside office, he manages talent old and new, and he keeps in touch with the "boys", as he still calls the now not-so-young but young-at-heart Wesleyan graduates he first approached at that General Artists' audition in November of 1959. Far away across the country is the newest member of the Highwaymen, Johann Helton at home in Idaho. In 2004 he released his third solo album, *Tell Me A Story*. It was recorded, like *The Water of Life* with the Highwaymen, at JoTown records, a division of his Goddess Sound Productions.

Nearby in Boise lives the Hon. Stephen S. Trott, Judge of the U.S. Ninth Circuit Court of Appeals. Although considered one of the few conservative judges on the notoriously liberal 9th Circuit, he has, in fact, often defied such simple characterization. While eloquent in dissent, he has at times taken positions opposed to what many might consider the "knee-jerk" conservative response, and he is an advocate of splitting the oversized and overwhelmed 9th Circuit into two more manageable territories. His oftime erudite decisions can include metaphors from *Alice's Adventures in Wonderland* among other literary or cultural references. He and Carol remain active in the community. In addition to his founding the Idaho Classical Guitar Society in 1990, Trott has been President of both the Boise Philharmonic Association and that city's Children's Home Society. He is the pre-concert lecturer for the Boise Philharmonic, occasionally performing the same service for the Seattle Symphony. He is also the official magician of the Children's Home. In November of 2004, the 65-year old jurist took Senior Status. He would go fishing, he said, having given up his youthful passion for golf), but more importantly intended to spend more time with his guitar, his mandolin, and his long-time colleagues performing and recording folk songs.

Trott's Wesleyan classmate and fellow attorney Robert Burnett lives in the east, where he and his wife Cathy (yes, the Colonel's daughter) reside in Riverside, Rhode Island. Bob Burnett was a Vice President at Bank of America, but after surviving a bout with brain cancer, he retired at the end of 2007. He and Cathy now like to spend time with their grandchildren and to host friendly sing-along gatherings at their home. So Bob Burnett's guitar is not far from this member of the original Highwaymen, and he cherishes his ongoing involvement with his folksinging compatriots.

After administrative stints at the University of Wisconsin in

Madison, Iowa's Grinnell College, and Lawrence University in Appleton, Wisconsin, Steve Butts has retired from academia and is living now in Kenosha, Wisconsin with his wife, Marian. His abiding passion is the 18th century baroque oboe. Butts' oboe d'amore, a mezzo-soprano instrument which first came into use around 1720, is featured on the Highwaymen's recent recording of "The Great Silkie". In addition to collecting and playing baroque oboes, the Highwaymen's bass singer and banjo player looks forward to the group's opportunities to come together in song.

Dave Fisher now resides full-time in Rye, New York, where Elaine remains in her position as Clinical Director of the Clearview School. Fisher's Highwaymen experience continues to have unforeseen ramifications and benefits. Cover versions of his "Santiano" arrangement have remained tremendous hits in France, particularly in recordings by the ever-popular Hugues Aufray. Beyond commercial releases, however, just a quick scan through youtube will find a number of amateur renditions of Fisher's "Santiano" in French, by fledgling performers of all ages. David Fisher is currently writing a book on singing method, but he also relishes those moments when he puts together CD tracks of new folk arrangements and sends them out to his friends so that they can practice and prepare.

A variety of venues—an outdoor stage just yards from Plymouth Rock, intimate folk-themed coffee houses, a thousand-seat amphitheater in Wisconsin, private halls and rented hotel banquet rooms—have been home to recent Highwaymen performances. From charity benefits in New England and California to Lincoln Center's Roots of American Music Festival in New York City, the group continues to share its special sound, expressing an abiding love for folk music, both old and new. The Highwaymen may get together only a couple of dozen times each year, but when they do they are ready to put on a show.

Former Highwaymen, too, continue to be creative and involved. While working as a contemporary choral director and following his son's screen career, Gil Robbins did not stray too far from his folk music roots. As recently as 2003, Gil Robbins arranged Jean Ritchie's song "My Dear Companion" for E. Henry David Music Publishers. Earlier, Robbins had arranged Ritchie's "Too Many Shadows", as well as an Indic Christmas Carol, "Lina Avatara (He Chose Birth Among Us)", for the same company. Meanwhile, Renny Temple continues to write screenplays. He was several times in contention for screenwriting competitions. He is also not far from his music. In the fall of 2000, for his 40th reunion at Walter Johnson High School in Bethesda, Maryland, Renny Temple wrote and sang a song which told the story of those four decades with humor and affection. Screenwriting and composing keeps Temple's former Highwaymen partner Mose Henry (nee Moses MacNaughten) busy as well. After finishing scoring a film in Oregon, he has begun work on a feature film project which he conceived and is writing. MacNaughten remembers his Highwaymen days fondly. "I will always be grateful," he says. "I really appreciate David Fisher giving me the chance to get started in a career I love." Roy Connors remains in advertising. Now living in Boca Raton, Florida, in September of 2005, he sent a letter to David Fisher, to update his old mentor on the intervening years. "I still play my 8-string guitar," Connors wrote,

> having sold my banjo years ago to a Japanese collector. And by the way, I never did learn how to 'frail'. I know you tried your best, I just couldn't get the hang of it.... You have no idea how

nostalgic I get whenever I see you guys on TV. Obviously, I've followed the group ever since being a part of it. Without question, it was the most exciting part of my life no matter what I've done since. And as my mother says, "How many people get the opportunity to do what I did?" I'm only sorry that I never got the opportunity to thank you for allowing me to be a part of it. Thank you.

Connors was able to say his "thank you" in person in December of 2007, when the original Highwaymen appeared at the Raymond F. Kravis Center for the Performing Arts in West Palm Beach.

Other old folk groups are still with us. The Limeliters, with newcomers Andy Corwin and Mack Bailey joining veteran Alex Hassilev, have developed a dynamic new website and have a new live CD available. They also schedule as many as thirty concert dates each year. After almost a half-century of performing with the Limeliters, Alex Hassilev began transitioning into a well-deserved retirement. Former New Christy Minstrel Gaylan Taylor has taken his place, although Hassilev joins the group onstage for special occasions. At the same time, former Limeliters Glenn Yarborough and Rick Dougherty teamed up with Dick Foley, a founding member of the Brothers Four, to tour as The Folk Reunion. Bill Zorn, another former Limeliter, returned to the Kingston Trio, filling in for an ailing Bob Shane. While Zorn, George Grove, and Bob Haworth toured as the Kingston Trio, Shane surprised a California audience in January of 2005, when he joined the group on stage to sing his signature solo, "Scotch and Soda". The current Kingston Trio consists of Grove, Zorn, and Zorn's old Limeliter compatriot Rick Dougherty. The Brothers Four appeared with the Kingston Trio and Folk Reunion for a series of live dates in the spring of 2005. The Shaw Brothers still perform together, on cruise ships, in church halls, and from bandstands on New England town greens. In January of 2006 they received the World Folk Music Association's Kate Wolf Award for 2005. The WFMA's Lifetime Achievement Award in 2006 went to Tom Paxton, who is still writing and singing songs. Likewise Bill Staines, who continues to tour and perform.

Peter, Paul, and Mary are back in action, now that Mary Travers has recovered from her cancer treatment. They perform maybe a dozen shows each year, with longtime bassist Richard Kniss (who co-wrote "Sunshine on my Shoulder" with John Denver) and the peripatetic Paul Prestopino backing them up instrumentally. Their musical director is Robert DeCormier, with whom Gil Robbins of the Highwaymen performed almost fifty years before.

The spirit of those halcyon days of the early sixties is also "still alive," says Steve Butts, "through the people who were active in that time and place who have gone on to other things." Woody Allen still makes movies, Martin Mull still makes jokes, Bill Cosby still makes headlines, and Simon and Garfunkel went back on tour together again. Folk musicians, notes Butts, "went into rock, into solo work, formed new groups... I think of it as a diaspora from the folk movement." It is clear, then, that the folk experience influenced so much of what was to follow.

As much as folk music is about the past, it is also about the future. There are so many new folk and folk-style artists performing today. Many of them are groups, and they appear in a variety of venues, representing diverse aspects of the folk genre. In Los Angeles, you might catch the traditional Irish sound of the Dublin 4, while in the Boston area you might hear the progressive folk offerings of the Maple Street Project, to give just two examples out of so many. And there are new folk sounds as well. "What is rap?"

asks Noel Paul Stookey. It is "Woody Guthrie's 'talking blues' down home, on the street," Stookey declares, answering his own question. He has a point. The phenomenon of rap fits most of Forcucci's eight criteria for authentic folk music: it tells a story, it is the musical expression of a people, it is colloquial, simply structured, effective when unaccompanied, and culturally indigenous. Only its frequently known authorship and its relative youth keep it from matching Forcucci's exact definition. Interestingly enough, though, is that so much of it is absorbed by ear and passed on by word of mouth that, a thousand years hence, rap could just possibly fulfill all the classic requirements. And if you get a chance, listen to the Limeliters' delightful "Folk Rap".

Poised somewhere between the nostalgia of the old and the energetic innovation of the new, are the four original Highwaymen. They have their claim on the past. With more than five million in sales to date, their version of "Michael" may be the most successful authentic traditional folk song recording of all time. In age and anonymity, in simplicity and effectiveness, in its cultural and colloquial roots, and in its narrative and history, it essentially fits Forcucci's description, and it remains the measure of the group's success. Yet the Highwaymen are not content to rest on their laurels. They are not a nostalgia act, nor do they allow themselves to be stifled by formal definitions. Their collaborations with other artists— bassist Johann Helton, singers Elaine Haagen and Cathy Burnett (all three, of course, integral members of the Highwaymen family) and violinists Richard Kriehn and Jeremy Gold—highlight their commitment to expanding their folk horizons. Their new website— www.originalhighwaymen.com—most surely asserts that they are part of the modern era, in tune with today. The Highwaymen have created a special children's show, in the tradition of the Limeliters' *Through Children's Eyes*, but far more intimate and personal. This new show features a delightful repertoire of songs old and new, and is highlighted by the prestidigitation and legerdemain of skilled magician Steve Trott, thereby gaining the original Highwaymen a whole new generation of younger fans.

In 2007, the Highwaymen released yet another new album. This CD, *When the Village Was Green*, was recorded live at the Blackstone River Theater in Cumberland, Rhode Island. Half of the songs on their newest CD are numbers new to the group since they first parted company in 1964. Indeed, this is also true of the forty-plus songs in their current repertoire. Among these is a David Fisher arranged medley of the Queenstown version of "Waltzing Matilda", combined with Eric Bogle's stirring "...And The Band Played Waltzing Matilda" (a tour de force for Steve Butts), and ending with the traditional version of the "unofficial Australian national anthem". Timely and powerful, this and other newly added songs demonstrate the group's commitment to remaining a living, vital folk music force.

Their earlier material has not been forgotten. Also in 2007, Varese Sarabande Vintage Records released a collection, entitled *The Highwaymen: The Folk Hits Collection*, featuring recordings from their entire career, including the previously unreleased "Old Folk Music... with some Sweet Rock n' Roll". Also previously unreleased was a newly remastered recording of a live Highwaymen concert from 1963, featuring Bob Burnett, Steve Butts, Chan Daniels, Dave Fisher, and Gil Robbins performing at M.I.T., which will come out on the Folk Era label in 2009.

Meanwhile, the original Highwaymen continue to perform and record music new and old, helping to keep the spirit of the Folk

Revival alive. Classic folk-style venues like the Town Crier Café in Pawling, NY, the Sounding Board in Hartford, CT, and Café Lena in Saratoga Springs have all been stops on the group's itinerary in 2008, along with the Highwaymen's usually sold-out appearances at the Guthrie Center in Massachusetts and the Blackstone River Theater in Rhode Island. In February of 2009, they will appear with Judy Collins at the McCallum Theater in Palm Desert, California, and in April of that year the original Highwaymen will undertake a 17-show West Coast Tour through California, Oregon, and Washington. This experience will recreate for the group the kind of adventure they lived as nationally-acclaimed folk artists almost half a century ago.

2008 was a tough year for folk music in many ways. January saw the passing of John Stewart, Gil Robbins' old singing partner, mainstay of the Cumberland Three and the later Kingston Trio, and a successful singer-songwriter in his own right. Ten months later, Nick Reynolds, one of the original, founding members of the Kingston Trio—the group that kicked off the "Great Folk Music Scare" in the midst of the modern 20th century "Folk Revival"—died. Then, in December, the folk world lost the incomparable Odetta. Amid these sad events, folk music lost other greats. Erik Darling— of the Tarriers, the Weavers, the Rooftop Singers—died in August, as did Ronnie Drew, that unique Irish voice from The Dubliners. The legendary Utah Phillips, Canadian Willie P. Bennett, and the versatile Artie Traum also left us during that time. With the passing of Hamilton Camp and Tommy Makem earlier in the decade, there are not many left from those early days to carry on the legacy of the Folk Revival.

But Pete Seeger, Arlo Guthrie, and Joan Baez all released new CDs in 2008. On Thanksgiving weekend, 2008, eighty-nine-year-old

Pete Seeger joined sixty-one year-old Arlo Guthrie with their families (including Arlo's daughter—and Woody's granddaughter—Sarah Lee Guthrie, her husband Johnny Irion, Annie Guthrie, Abe Guthrie, Pete's grandson Tao Rodriguez Seeger, and more) onstage at Carnegie Hall, to sing songs both old and new.

Old songs, like the labor classics sung by Seeger and Arlo's father close to seventy years ago, are celebrated by newer artists—like the DC Labor Chorus and its like-minded ensembles around the nation—and echoed by contemporary songwriters such as Paul McKenna. There are new sounds, as well, from newer artists, such as Janet Feld, Howie Newman, Beth DeSombre, Kelly Moore, Sometymes Why, Halali, Angel Band, the Maple Street Project, Frank Carillo with the Bandoleros, Mary McCaslin, Lori McKenna, Mary Gauthier, and so many more, all—like the Highwaymen—carrying on the folk tradition.

And that tradition was powerfully represented on inauguration day, 2009, when Pete Seeger performed on the steps of the Lincoln Memorial, joined by his grandson Tao and friend Bruce Springsteen, to lead the assembled multitudes—including President Barack Obama—in Woody Guthrie's "This Land Is Your Land."

Like Dar Williams, originally a Joan Baez protégé, who in 2008 released her latest CD, *Promised Land*, all these artists are enriching the legacy of the Folk Revival with their efforts in the progressive folk genre. Williams' roots, of course, were in that cradle of ethnomusicology, Connecticut's Wesleyan University, just like the original Highwaymen.

The Highwaymen continue to add new songs into their repertoire. Cathy Burnett now joins her husband on stage to sing Bill Staines' "Child of Mine". The newest song by Tommy Sands—a tribute to the late Tommy Makem—is now a fixture of Highwaymen concerts. Their children's show—replete with music, magic, and merriment— continues to thrive and expand. Songs like "Dancing with Bears" by Dr. Seuss, along with "Big Rock Candy Mountain", "Place In The Choir", and Steve Trott's prestidigitations now entertain a new generation of budding folk aficionados.

The music of the Highwaymen is like all folk music—capturing echoes of yesterday while resonating with today and celebrating the hope offered by tomorrow. Their music—like all folk music—is forever.

APPENDIX A

Discography

*Bob Burnett-Steve Butts-Chan Daniels-David Fisher-Steve Trott

45 Michael/SantianoUA 258released 9-21-1960

LP *The Highwaymen* (UAL-3125/UAS-6125) produced by Don Costa *
released Jan. 1961

> Santiano; Big Rock Candy Mountain; A La Claire Fontaine: Carni
> Valito; Ah Si Mon Moine; Sinner Man/ Michael; Take This
> Hammer; Au Claire De La Lune; Greenland Fisheries; Irish Work
> Song (Pat Works on the Railway); Cindy, O Cindy.

> *Boston-born Don Costa was a veteran producer who helped*
> *make stars of Paul Anka ("Diana", "Lonely Boy") and Trini*
> *Lopez ("If I Had a Hammer"). He produced the first three*
> *Highwaymen albums and all of their first four singles except*
> *"Bird Man". He was also under the management of Ken*
> *Greengrass, although Dave Fisher would state that Costa was*
> *"irrepressibly unmanageable".*

45 The Gypsy Rover/Cotton FieldsUA 370released 10-09-1961

LP *Standing Room Only* (UAL-3168/UAS 6168) produced by Don
Costa * released Nov. 1961

> Cotton Fields; Black-Eyed Suzie; Rise Up Shepherd;

Nostalgias Tucumanas; Three Jolly Rogues; Pollerita/The Gypsy Rover; The Calton Weaver; Wildwood Flower; Johnny with the Bandy Legs; The Great Silkie; Run Come See Jerusalem

45 I'm On My Way/Whisky in the JarUA 439released 2-23-1962

LP *Encore* (UAL-3225/UAS-6225) produced by Don Costa/GLG Productions * released May 1962* cover by Frank Guana

Whisky in the Jar; Bim Bam; Eres Alta; Railroad Bill; Fiesta Linda; Little Boy; Lonesome Road Blues/I'm On My Way; Die Moorsoldaten; Ballad of Spring Hill; El Rancho Grande; Fare Thee O Babe; Mighty Day

5 Cindy O Cindy/The Bird ManUA 475released 6-25-1962

*While "Cindy O Cindy" came from the group's debut album and was produced by Don Costa, "The Bird Man" was written (with Dave Fisher) and produced by Elmer Bernstein, with Burt Lancaster doing the narration, for the film **Birdman of Alcatraz**. It was never used in the picture.*

*Steve Butts-Chan Daniels-Dave Fisher-Gil Robbins

45 I Know Where I'm Going/Well, Well, Well UA 540released 10-10-1962

LP *March On, Brothers* (UAL-3245/UAS-6245) produced by Milt Okun * released Nov. 1962

March On, Brothers!; I Never Will Mary; Away, Love, Away; The Devil's Away; Marianne; I'll Fly Away/(Marching to) Pretoria; I Know Where I'm Going;Viva Jujuy;Well, Well, Well; John; One Man's Hands

This LP and the two singles (UA 540, UA 568) that came from it were produced by Milt Okun, the man who put Peter, Paul & Mary together and who discovered and produced much of John Denver's work. Okun was also a recipient of the John Denver Award from the WFMA.

45 (Marching to) Pretoria/I Never Will MarryUA 568released 1-10-1963

*Although these songs appeared on the **March On, Brothers** LP, both of these recordings feature versions different from the album cuts. This is especially true of "Pretoria", which on the single has a driving drumbeat backing the voices.*

*Bob Burnett-Steve Butts-Chan Daniels-Dave Fisher-Gil Robbins

45 All My Trials/Midnight TrainUA 602released May 1963

This is the group's "lost" single. As "All My Trials" never appeared on an album and "Midnight Train" would not be used

on an LP until later, it is relatively rare. If not for the subsequent **One More Time!** *LP and for the EMI Legendary Masters Series, these songs would truly have been lost.*

LP *Hootenanny with the Highwaymen* (UAL-3294/UAS-6294) a GLG Production. *
    produced by Nick Peritoreleased June 1963
    mixed by Gil Robbins and Dave Fisher

Roll On, Columbia, Roll On; Raise a Ruckus Tonight; The Old Maid's Song; Shaggy Dog Songs; The Tale of Michael Flynn; The Turtle Dove; Michael & Cotton Fields/Passing Through; Mister Noah; La Canzone Del Vino; Can Ye Sew Cushions; Chanson de Chagrin; One for the Money; You're Always Welcome at Our House; Roll On, Columbia, Roll On (reprise).

GLG Productions was a company formed by manager Ken Greengrass and his clients Steve Lawrence and Eydie Gorme (Greengrass-Lawrence-Gorme – GLG).

45 Universal Soldier/I'll Fly AwayUA 647released Sept. 1963
LP *One More Time!* (UAL-3323/UAS-6323) a GLG Production *
    produced by Fred Hellerman *
    released October 1963

* cover design by Norman Art Studio

Universal Soldier; Work of the Weavers; The Lady Bug & the Centipede; Ayaman Ibo Lele; Abilene; So Fare Ye Well/La Bamba; The First Time (Ever I Saw Your Face); Sourwood Mountain; Shabbat Shalom; Poor Old Man; Midnight Train.

45 The Tale of Michael Flynn/Roll On, Columbia UA 679released December 1963

45 The Sinking of the Reuben James/Bon SoirUA 695released January 1964

> *This is a studio single, although it features two songs which came out later that year on their live **Homecoming!** LP.*

LP *Homecoming!* (UAL-3348/UAS-6348) produced by Bernie Krause for GLG Productions *

Recording Engineer: Tory Brainerd * released April 1964

Standing by the Gate; Gypsy Rover; There Comes Alibama; Shotgun Talking Blues; Rhody; Careless Love; The Sinking of the Reuben James/Brandy is my True Love's Name; Riddles; Jenny's Gone and I Don't Care; Did You Ever See a Wild Goose?; Morning Dew; 'Possum Meat; Bon Soir (Le Roi Des Buveurs).

45 Sweet Mama, Treetop Tall/ NellieUA 752released 7-6-1964

> *This single was produced by Jerry Ragovoy, and featured only*

the Highwaymen singing, with studio musicians playing the instruments. One of these was Eric Weissberg, accomplished on both the banjo and the bass. Highwaymen banjoist Steve Butts is a great admirer of Weissberg, who has an extensive discography and is perhaps most famous for the "Dueling Banjos" of Deliverance fame. Weissberg once wrote that his greatest musical influence was Ricard Wagner. Not bad for a folk musician/banjo player with a Julliard education.

LP *The Spirit & The Flesh* (UAL-3397/UAS-6397) a GLG Production * produced and mixed by Gil Robbins and David Fisher * released October 1964

Pharoh's Army-Old Time Religion; Well, Well, Well; John; One More River; I'll Fly Away; Come Down, Gabriel/Nothing More to Look Forward To; Doney Gal; Pretty Mary; April is in My Mistress' Face; When the World Was Young; Rambling Boy.

Dave Fisher-Chan Daniels

45 Michael '65/Puttin' On The StyleUA 801released 11-12-1964

This single featured the Dick Williams Singers essentially backing up Dave Fisher and Chan Daniels. It was produced by Don Costa and Ken Greengrass, and featured Eric Weissberg (see note above) on the banjo.

ABC-PARAMOUNT

Dave Fisher directing/Ken Greengrass managing

Roy Connors-Mose Henry-Alan Shaw-Renny Temple

45 Should I Go, Should I Stay/Permit to be a HermitABC 10688released 6-3-1965

LP *On a New Road* (ABC/ABCS-522) produced by Bob Crewe for GLG Productions * releasedAugust 1965

> Arranged & conducted by Charles Calello * Musical Director: David Fisher
>
> Cover design & photos by ARW Productions, Inc.

> On A New Road; You Won't Last Long in This Town; I'll Show You the Way; Follow Me (If You Would); Girls; Permit to be a Hermit/Another World; Dreams Like Sand; Never a Thought for Tomorrow; Smile at Me; I'll Be Gone; Should I Go, Should I Stay?

45 I'll Show You The Way/Never a Thought for Tomorrow ABC 10716 released 8-19-1965

LP *Stop! Look! & Listen!* (ABC/ABCS-543) produced by David Fisher for GLG Productions *

> released February 1966
>
> Arrangements by David Fisher * Production Supervisor: Ken Greengrass *
>
> Sound Engineer: Phil Ramone * Cover Design by ARW Productions, Inc. *
>
> Liner Design by Joe Lebow

> Bright Golden Buttons; A Taste of Honey; Cripple Creek; What's That I Hear?; Gotta Travel On; Sing Some More/Sing On Brothers; Whoa Mule Whoa; Trouble in Mind; Green, Green Rocky Road; Old Blue; Bonny Heilan' Laddie.

45 She's Not There/Little Bird, Little Bird ABC 10801 released 3-31-1966

45 My Foolish Pride/FlameABC 10824 released 6-13-1966

ORION of Canada

Chan Daniels-Dave Fisher-Steve Trott

45 Michael/ "Number #1"Orion 7403released Sept. 1974

This last was produced by Chan Daniels at Capitol Records.

EMI-Capitol

CD *Michael Row the Boat Ashore: the best of the Highwaymen* released 1992

A compilation of 24 songs by the original Highwaymen. Part of the EMI Legendary Masters Series.

CD Back 2 Back Hitsreleased 1997

An EMI-Capitol compilation, featuring five Kingston Trio hits and five songs from the Highwaymen (including the rare"Bird Man)".

CD *Two Classic Albums from The Highwaymen* released 2000

A re-release on CD of the first two original Highwaymen LPs— ***The Highwaymen*** *and* ***Standing Room Only!*** *An EMI-Capitol Music release for Collector's Choice Music.*

INDEPENDENTLY PRODUCED (dayfish music – dayfish@earthlink.net)

Bob Burnett-Steve Butts-Dave Fisher-Steve Trott, with Johann Helton on bass

CD *Still Rowing* newly recorded and mastered by Dave Fisher, Universal Studios,Los Angeles, California

released 1999

> Irene Goodnight; I Know Where I'm Going; Whiskey in the Jar; The Work of the Weavers; When the Village Was Green; La Bamba; The Gypsy Rover; The Glory Years; Michael; Number #1.

> > *The 1999 date is arbitrary—it was recorded and put together throughout the decade, beginning in the early '90s. David Fisher and the author disagree about the final cut, "Number #1". He says it is a new version of the song. I swear it is the 1974 recording, perhaps remastered, but otherwise the same, and that the late Chan Daniels **can** be heard on the track.*

CD *The Highwaymen: In Concert* recorded live in New York, Connecticut, and Idaho

compiled by Steve Butts

mastered by Don Cunningham and Johann Helton

at Cunningham Audio in Boise, Idaho.

released 2003

Santianno; The Gypsy Rover; Irish Work Song; Introductions-Highwaymen Name Story; A Place in the Choir; Red is the Rose; The River; The Tale of Michael Flynn; Streets of Laredo; The Sinking of the Reuben James; The Other Highwaymen Story; Wild Goose-Greenland Fisheries; Finnegan's Wake; Ramblin' Boy talk; Ramblin' Boy; Guantanamera; La Bamba; Michael; Cotton Fields; The Parting Glass.

with Johann Helton on bass.

CD *The Water of Life: a Celtic Collection* engineered by Johann Helton at JoTown Records,Boise, Idaho

mastered by Dave Fisher and Don Cunningham at Cunningham Audio, Boise, Idaho

cover photograph by Steve Butts

released 2004

Down by the Lagan Side; Ramblin' Rover-The Gypsy Rover; Nancy Whiskey; Paddy's Lamentation; Paddy Works on the Railway; Red is the Rose; Irish Lamentation Waltz; Whiskey in the Jar; The Great Silkie; Work of the Weavers; Broom of the Cowdenknowes; Finnegan's Wake; Parting Glass.

with Johann Helton on bass, Richard Kriehn on violin, and Elaine Haagen on vocals for "The Great Silkie".

CD *"When the Village Was Green" Live from the Blackstone River Theater*

engineered by Doug Brunelle (sound) and

Laurence Coch (in Rhode Island)

mastered and mixed at Cunningham Audio

Productions, Boise, Idaho

released in 2007

Roll On, Columbia, Roll On; Ramblin' Rover; Daughters and Sons; The Queen of Connemara; Big Rock Candy Mountain; Ashokan Farewell; Manchester Rambler; The Jolly Swagman/And The Band Played waltzing Matilda/Waltzing Matilda; El Humahuaqueno; The Glory Years; Roll Turn Spin (instrumental); Green, Green Rocky Road; When the Village Was Green; The Water is Wide/Fair and Tender Ladies; Work of the Weavers; Goodnight, Irene.

Johann Helton on bass

Jeremy Gold on violin

Varese Sarabande/Varese Vintage records

CD *The Highwaymen: The Folk Hits Collection*   released in 2007

A collection of Highwaymen folk recordings from 1961-2007, including the rare "Old Folk Music (With Some Sweet Rock n' Roll)" from 1974-75.

Folk Era Records

soon-to-be (if not already) released **CD** *The Highwaymen*

Live at MIT (working title) released in 2009

> *A newly remastered version of a previously unreleased "lost"*
> *Highwaymen concert from 1963, at the Massachusetts Institute*
> *of Technology, featuring Bob Burnett, Steve Butts, Chan*
> *Daniels, Dave Fisher, and Gil Robbins.*

Disc 1: March On Brothers; I'll Fly Away; The Gypsy Rover: Pretoria; Marianne: Shaggy Dog Songs; Roll On, Columbia; Portland County Jail (Tale of Michael Flynn); El Humahuaqueno (Carnivalito); La Bamba; Well, Well, Well; The Lady Bug and the Centipede; The Sinking of the Reuben James: Michael; Cotton Fields

Disc 2: John; I Know Where I'm Going; Sourwood Mountain; Little Boy; Mr. Noah; Canzone Del Vino; Abilene; Passing Through; Aunt Rhody; I Never Will Marry; So Fare Ye Well; You're Always Welcome At Our House; Midnight Train; Universal Soldier

APPENDIX B

Number One Folk Hits
and Folk Group chart successes

This is not a definitive analysis. The purpose of this Appendix is to show what folk groups had Number One hits from 1950-1965, as well as to discover other chart successes by folk groups in the same period. There are a number of assumptions about the last Folk Revival and "The Great Folk Music Scare" that have never been really examined. Finally, some attention will be paid to the successors of the folk revival—the Folk rockers and their ilk—to see what folk-rooted chart successes continued as the decade of the sixties came to a close.

FOLK REVIVAL

While the Almanac Singers in the early forties were the first modern folk "group", along with the recording/broadcasting only Union Boys, neither were fully styled for popular or commercial success. In the late forties, any folk music with commercial popularity came from solo artists. Burl Ives scored chart hits from 1940-1947 with "Wayfaring Stranger", "The Foggy, Foggy Dew", and "Big Rock Candy Mountain". He had a Top 10 hit with "Blue Tail Fly" in 1948 (originally with the Andrews Sisters), and the following year he charted again with "Lavender's Blue (Dilly Dilly)". That same year (1949) the first commercially popular folk group—the Weavers—was formed.

1950—"Irene Goodnight" by the Weavers (with Gordon Jenkins and his orchestra) held the #1 position on the charts for 13 weeks, and was the #1 U.S. hit song for the entire year. The song ultimately reached close to 2 million in sales, at a time before there were "Gold Records" awarded.

"Tzena, Tzena" by the Weavers (with Gordon Jenkins and his orchestra) reached #2 on the charts and was the 13th best-selling song of the entire year.

1951—"On Top of Old Smokey" by the Weavers (with Gordon Jenkins, et al) reached #2 on the charts and was the #6 song the overall year, selling more than a million records.

1952—"Wimoweh" by the Weavers made the Top 40, selling a million records.

From 1952-1957 no folk songs reached #1 on the charts.

From 1952-1953 there were no songs by folk groups in the end-of-year overall Top 40 rankings.

1954—"Sylvie" by the Weavers did reach #27 for a brief time.

In 1955 there were no songs by folk groups in the end-of-year Top 40 rankings. The Weavers' Carnegie Hall Reunion LP sold extremely well, however.

During the early-to-mid 1950s, Burl Ives charted with "Riders in the

Sky", "On Top of Old Smoky", "The Wild Side of Life", etc., but none made the end of year rankings.

In 1956, Lonnie Donegan's "Rock Island Line" reached #8 on the charts and #50 overall for the year, but no folk group charted successfully.

Tennessee Ernie Ford's "Sixteen Tons"—essentially a country song, was 29th best for the year, and Harry Belafonte did have two LPs among the year's Top Ten albums.

Banana Boat Song" by the Tarriers was the 26th most successful song of the year (the first folk trio to achieve chart success) but it was overshadowed by Harry Belafonte's "Day-O" version of the same song, which reached #2 and was ranked #15 on the year. Solo artists like Belafonte did well in 1957: Jimmie Rodgers' "Kisses Sweeter Than Wine" reached #3, while Belafonte had a #14 hit in "Jamaica Farewell".

1957—"Marianne" by Terry Gilkyson and the Easy Riders reached #4 on the charts and #37 overall for the year.

"THE GREAT FOLK MUSIC SCARE"

1958—"Tom Dooley" by the Kingston Trio reaches #1 on the charts and is ranked #24th on the year overall. In its first year of release, the song sells morethan 2 million records. Eventually, more than three million copies of "Tom Dooley" will be sold.

No other folk songs charted in 1958.

1959—"Tijuana Jail" by the Kingston Trio reaches #12 on the charts.

"(Charlie on the) M.T.A." by the Kingston Trio reaches #15 on the charts.

"A Worried Man" by the Kingston Trio reaches #20 on the charts.

This is definitely the year of the Kingston Trio ("Tom Dooley" remains on the charts as well), and the "Great Folk Music Scare" is off and running. Not only did they have several different singles on the charts in 1959, but the Kingston Trio also had five different albums in the Top 10. In fact (see below) the Kingston Trio were the first group ever to have stronger LP sales than single sales (eventually 14 of their albums would make the Top 40). The Kingston Trio won two Grammy Awards in 1959. That same year, the only other folk artist to chart significantly was Billy Grammer, who briefly reached #4 with "Gotta Travel On". Johnny Horton's quasi-folk/country historical pastiche, "Battle of New Orleans", was the #2nd ranked song overall that year, however.

1960—"Greenfields" by the Brothers Four reached #2 on the charts and was the #13th ranked song overall on the year. It sold over a million records its first year, and close to two million overall. Their first two albums also charted.

Although several Kingston Trio songs charted, none made the Top 40 in 1960, although three Kingston Trio albums did.

1961—"Michael" by the Highwaymen reached #1 on the charts and was the 2nd most successful song of the year overall. In its first full year of release it sold two-and-a-half million records, and it would eventually reach five million-plus in sales.

"Santiano" by the Highwaymen charted at #100.

"Cindy, O Cindy" by the Highwaymen charted at #42.

"Big Rock Candy Mountain" by the Highwaymen charted at #42.

The group's first album also charted.

"A Dollar Down" by the Limeliters reaches #60 on the charts. They also did very well with album sales.

"The Green Leaves of Summer" by the Brothers Four did make the charts, at #41, but it had its greatest success when it was nominated for an Academy Award (the film was *The Alamo*).

"Frogg" by the Brothers Four did reach #32 on the charts, albeit briefly.

That same year, the Kingston Trio continued to excel at album sales, while former folksinger turned country/pop artist and actor Burl Ives took his "Little Bitty Tear" to #9. Also in 1961, Harry Belafonte's live album *At Carnegie Hall* was the 10th best selling LP of the year. 1962—"Cotton Fields" by the Highwaymen reached #13, and it spent over three months on the charts, earning its ranking as the 36th

most successful song that year overall. It sold a million records in one year, and eventually reached two million in sales. No other folk song made the end-of-year Top 40.

"The Gypsy Rover" by the Highwaymen reached #42 on the charts.

"Three Jolly Rogues" by the Highwaymen charted at #99.

"The Calton Weaver" by the Highwaymen charted at #99.

"I'm On My Way" by the Highwaymen charted at #90.

The group's second album also charted.

"Blue Water Line" by the Brothers Four reached #50 on the charts.

"The Reverend Mr. Black" by the Kingston Trio reached #8 on the charts.

"Where Have all the Flowers Gone" by the Kingston Trio reached #21.

"Scotch & Soda" by the Kingston Trio reached #81 in Billboard's Hot 100.

The Trio's LPs continued to sell extremely well.

"Lizzie Borden" by the Chad Mitchell Trio reached #44.
"I Had a Mule" by the Limeliters reached #25 on the charts.

"The Riddle Song" by the Limeliters reached #25.

"Funk" by the Limeliters reached #21. The group's LP sales were terrific.

Also, the folk/country Springfields reached #20 with "Silver Threads and Golden Needles", while Burl Ives' "Funny Way of Laughing" reached #10. He would also chart with "Call Me Mr. In-Between." The 10th best selling LP of the year was *Vol. 2* from Joan Baez.

1963—"Walk Right In" by the Rooftop Singers reached #1 on the charts and was the 34th most successful song in 1963.

"Mama Don't 'Low" by the Rooftop Singers charted at #55.

"Puff, the Magic Dragon" by Peter, Paul, & Mary reached #2 on the charts and was ranked #15th overall that year.

"Blowin' in the Wind" by Peter, Paul, & Mary reached #2 on the charts and was the #32nd ranked song of 1963. Peter, Paul, & Mary's first two albums—*Peter, Paul & Mary* and *Movin'*—were the 2nd and 3rd bestselling LPs of the year in 1963 (*In Concert* by Joan Baez was 4th). More than a dozen other songs by PP&M would make it into Billboard's Hot 100 over the next few years (19 in all, including their #1 hit in 1969).

"Green, Green" by the New Christy Minstrels reached #14 on the charts.

"Saturday Night" by the New Christy Minstrels charted at #29.

Early LP sales by the New Christy Minstrels were also good.

"Greenback Dollar" by the Kingston Trio reached #21. This was the last of eleven chart singles for the Kingston Trio.

"The Midnight Special" by the Limeliters reached #73. Another Limeliter song,

"A Casinha-Pequenina (Little House)" finished just out of the Billboard Hot 100.

"The Tale of Michael Flynn" by the Highwaymen charted at #79. This was the last of ten chart singles for the Highwaymen. The group's fifth album—*Hootenanny with the Highwaymen*—also charted.

While in many ways 1963 was the pinnacle of "The Great Folk Music Scare", it was also the beginning of its downslide. Overall sales were on the decline, and soon the Kingston Trio would be without a record label. Still, there were other folk or semi-folk successes that year. "Dominique" by the Singing Nun reached #1, "If I Had a Hammer" by Trini Lopez made it to #3, as did "Tie Me Kangaroo Down Sport" by Laurinda Almeida and the Bossa Nova All Stars. "Abilene" by George Hamilton IV reached #15.

1964—"Don't Let the Rain Come In" by the Serendipity Singers reached #6 on the charts, and was #32 on the year overall.

"Today" by the New Christy Minstrels reached #17.

"The Marvelous Toy" by the Chad Mitchell Trio charted at #43.

Two Peter, Paul, & Mary albums—*Blowin' in the Wind* and *PP&M*—were again among the year's Top 10 bestselling LPs overall. Another Limeliters song, "No Man is an Island" finished just out of the Billboard Hot 100. Also: "Little Boxes" by Pete Seeger at #70, "Winken Blinken & Nod" by The Simon Sisters at #73, "We'll Sing in the Sunshine" by Gale Garnett at #4, and "Summer Song" (#7) and "Yesterday's Gone" (#21) by Chad & Jeremy. Folk artists like Ian & Sylvia ("Someday Soon") released good songs which did not chart. From the old to the new: the folk rock era was about to begin.

FOLK-ROCK ERA

1965—"Tambourine Man" by the Byrds reached #1 and was 28th on the year overall.

"Turn, Turn" by the Byrds reached #1 and was 52nd on the year overall.

"You Were On My Mind" by We Five reached #3 and was the 4th most successful song overall that year.

"I'll Never Find Another You" by the Seekers reached #4.

Also: Barry McGuire's "Eve of Destruction" at #1 (29th overall),
Bob Dylan's "Like a Rolling Stone" at #2 (41st overall), "Catch the
Wind" by Donovan at #23, and "Baby the Rain Must Fall" by ex-
Limeliter Glenn Yarborough at #12. Other 1965 with folk roots
included "It Ain't Me Babe" by the Turtles (written by Bob Dylan) at
#8, "Do You Believe in Magic" by the Lovin' Spoonful (with John
Sebastian) at #9, "King of the Road" by Roger Miller at #4, "I Go to
Pieces" by Peter & Gordon, "Laugh, Laugh" by the Beau Brummels
at #15, and "All I Really Want to Do" by Cher (written by Bob
Dylan) at #15.

1966—"California Dreamin'" by the Mamas & the Paoas reached #4
on the charts, and was the 25th ranked song overall at year's end.

"Monday, Monday" by the Mamas & the Papas reached #1 on the
charts and was was ranked #13 overall on the year. Their debut
album—"If You Can't Believe Your Eyes and Ears" was the 7th
bestselling album of 1966.

"Red Rubber Ball" by Cyrkle (a song written by Paul Simon)
reached the Top 40 in 1966 and was the 34th ranked song that year.
"The Sounds of Silence" by Simon & Garfunkel reached #1 on the
charts and was the 20th ranked song in 1966.

"Time" by the Pozo-Seco Singers reached #47 on the charts.
Bob Lind reached #5 with "Elusive Butterfly". Also in 1966: Bobby
Darrin's "If I Were a Carpenter" at #8, "La Bamba" by Trini Lopez
at #86, and Staff Sgt. Barry Sadler's "Ballad of the Green Berets"
(#1 on the charts and for the year).

248

1967—"For What It's Worth" by Buffalo Springfield charted in the Top 40, and was the 26th ranked song overall that year.

"Georgy Girl" by the Seekers reached #2 on the charts and was ranked 24th overall on the year.

"Creeque Alley" by the Mamas & the Papas charted in the Top 40.

"59th Street Bridge Song (Feelin' Groovy)" by Harper's Bizarre reached #13 (it was written by Paul Simon).

"Let's Live for Today" by the Grass Roots reached #8 on the charts.

"Windy" by the Association (#1 & #5 overall) and "Happy Together" by the Turtles (#1, #8 overall) featured performers with folk roots. Other folk-rock or folk-rooted successors in 1967 included "San Francisco" by Scott McKenzie (formerly of the Journeymen) which Reached #1 briefly and was #45 overall, and perhaps even "Ode to Billie Joe" by Bobbie Gentry (#1, #3 overall).

1968—"The Unicorn" by the Irish Rovers reached #7 on the charts.

"Mrs. Robinson" by Simon & Garfunkel reached #1 and was ranked in the year's Top 10 overall. Two Simon & Garfunkel albums— "Parsley, Sage, Rosemary, and Thyme" and "Bookends" were among the Top 10 bestselling LPs of 1968.

"The Weight" by the Band reached #63 on the charts.

Michael Nesmith's "Different Drum" recorded by Linda Ronstadt and the Stone Poneys reached #13 on the charts. Other folk-rooted artists with songs on the charts in 1968 included "Light My Fire" by Jose Feliciano at #3, "Mr. Bojangles" by Jerry Jeff Walker at #77, "Reach Out of the Darkness" by Friend & Lover at #10, as well as songs by the Lemon Pipers, the Grass Roots, etc. "Abraham, Martin, and John" by Dion reached #4. Richie Havens recorded Bob Dylan's "Just Like a Woman" in 1968, but it did not chart.

1969—"Day is Done" by Peter, Paul & Mary made the Top 40.

"Leaving on a Jet Plane" by Peter, Paul & Mary reached #1 on the charts and was the 50th ranked song that year. It was written by John Denver.

"Ruby, Don't Take Your Love to Town" by Kenny Rogers and the First Edition reached #6 on the charts.

"Get Together" by the Youngbloods reached #5 on the charts.

Also in 1969: "Everybody's Talkin'" by Harry Nilsson at #6, "Galveston" by Glenn Campbell at #4, and "Love is Just a Four Letter Word" by Joan Baez at #86 (written by Bob Dylan).

THE MODERN ERA

In this period, Simon & Garfunkel, Paul Simon, John Denver—they all had hits. The Modern Era moved from folk-rock to the age of the singer-songwriter: Carole King, Don McLean, Jonathan Edwards, James Taylor, etc. During this time, however, there were a few more traditional folk or folk-style songs: some charted and some did not. A few examples:

1970—"Universal Soldier" by Buffy St. Marie did not chart.

1971—'Brand New Key" by Melanie reached #1 for one week.

1983—"Light One Candle" by Peter, Paul & Mary (written by Peter Yarrow) did not chart, however it is ranked among Billboard's Top 10 Traditional Holiday Songs ever.

****

What follows is not a complete or comprehensive list, but the intention is to give the reader an accurate sense of commercial success for folk groups during this time. There is no question, based on all the available resources, that the Kingston Trio (11 singles charting, a Number One hit, 2 Grammy Awards, and 14 Top 40 albums) and Peter, Paul, & Mary (19 singles charting, a Number One hit, 3 Grammy Awards—and numerous Grammy and Emmy nominations—and 8 Top 40 albums) are the two most successful folk groups of all time. To break it down by category (and keeping in mind that the statistics is an inexact science and can always stand revising):

Singles Success

1. Peter, Paul, & Mary (19 charted songs with one #1 hit) [some AFTER 1965, w/ #1]

.2. The Kingston Trio (11 with one #1 hit)

3. The Highwaymen (10 with one #1 hit))

4. The Weavers (6 with one #1 hit))

5. Brothers Four (5)

6. The New Christy Minstrels (5)

7. The Limeliters (5)

8. The Rooftop Singers (2 with one #1 hit)

9. Chad Mitchell Trio (4)

10. The Tarriers (2)

11. The Serendipity Singers (2)

Album (LP or CD) Success

1. The Kingston Trio (14 charted albums)

2. Peter, Paul & Mary (8)

3. The Limeliters (6)

4. The Weavers (5)

5. The New Christy Minstrels (4)

6. Brothers Four, and the Highwaymen (3 each)

7. The Chad Mitchell Trio (2)

8. Schooner Fare [CDs, well after '65, from '76 on]

Overall Recording Success

The distinction between the top three on this list is at best a semantic one—depending on whether you prioritize total chart appearances, volume of sales, or percentage of success; all, of course, dependent upon era. They are, in whatever order you choose, the three most successful folk groups of all time.

1. Peter, Paul, & Mary (27 overall chart appearances—**singles & albums**—17 TOP 40 with one at #1) [and noting that some of this was AFTER 1965, including their #1 hit]
2. The Kingston Trio (25 overall chart appearances – 23 TOP 40 with two at #1)
3. The Weavers (11 overall – ALL TOP 40 with two #1)
4. The Highwaymen (13 – 3 TOP 40 and one #1)
5. The Limeliters (11 – 6 TOP 40)
6. The Brothers Four (8 – 4 TOP 40)
7. The New Christy Minstrels (9 – 3 TOP 40)
8. The Chad Mitchell Trio (6 – 2 TOP 40)
9. The Rooftop Singers (3 – 1 TOP 40 & one #1)

*For all this, out of the roughly 4000 songs which made it into Billboard's Hot 100 between 1958-1965, only about 400 were folk songs (roughly 10%), and fewer than 100 came from folk **groups**. Rock n' Roll and Pop still overwhelmingly dominated the singles charts during that time (although film soundtrack and Broadway cast albums held a slight edge on the album charts). The recording industry had very little, then, to fear from folk music—especially folk groups—in the early sixties. But folk acts—with their appeal to college audiences and their relatively low overhead costs—were cutting in to the Caravans and individual record label tours that had been a staple of rock n' roll and pop performers since the mid-fifties. "The Great Folk Music Scare", it seems, was far more about live concert performance than it was about record sales.*

****

It is much harder to determine live appearance/concert success. The Kingston Trio were an unprecedented and unparalleled phenomenon when they first burst on the scene. Peter, Paul, & Mary have drawn bigger crowds since, but not for as many dates a year as the Kingston Trio had in their prime. Every one of these groups has broken up for a while before starting up again, except for the Brothers Four, which has performed continuously now for forty-seven years, with particular success more recently overseas, especially in Japan. Schooner Fare, on the other hand, played to packed houses over the better part of two decades, albeit often in smaller venues.

What follows is my best-educated guess ranking which folk groups have experienced the greatest live concert success over the years:

Live Concert Success (much of which continues to this day)

1. The Kingston Trio
2. Peter, Paul, & Mary
3. The Brothers Four
4. The Weavers and the Limeliters
5. The Chad Mitchell Trio
6. The New Christy Minstrels
7. Schooner Fare
8. The Highwaymen
9. The Tarriers
10. The Journeymen

All this, of course, does not include individual folk artists and folk or folk-style duos. It also begs the contrast between the more traditional, "purist" folk acts and the more popular commercial groups. Still, this distinction seems to have muted somewhat, as the surviving veterans of "The Great Folk Music Scare" have moved past the sometimes startlingly huge commercial success of those years and are more and more being recognized as traditional performers on the current folk scene. And whether you're stunned by an unexpected million-plus selling hit ("Tom Dooley", "Michael") or busking from town to town like Woody Guthrie and Ramblin' Jack Elliott, you're not in it for nothing. As Lou Gottlieb of the Limeliters once said, "This is the kind of music which brought us perilously close to solvency."

Just as the distinction between modern folk-style songs (what Forcucci calls "modern urban folk") and the older, more "authentic" folk music (see Forcucci's eight criteria) has become effectively blurred in recent times, so should the sometimes acrimonious debates between traditional folk purists and the commercial folk scene be brought to an end. Perhaps the reason that the" folk community refuses to take responsibility for defining folk music" is that it defies definition. Perhaps Mark Moss is right, in allowing the broadest parameters for folk music. It is, after all, the one genre of music where elitism of any kind has no place. Folk music is everyone's and anyone's music.

APPENDIX C

Folk Connections – the folk groups

While the rest of us may indulge ourselves in discovering "six degrees of separation", in the folk music world, particularly the 20th century folk revival and commercial folk scene, relationships might more accurately be measured by degrees of connection. You can think of the list below as a kind of a linear family tree, if you will, with the various connecting branches referenced in parentheses. You will not find much about folk duos (Ian & Sylvia, Bud & Travis, the Smothers Brothers, etc.) or solo artists emphasized here. It focuses, as previously noted, primarily on folk groups. Enjoy!

Woody Guthrie

begat

THE ALMANAC SINGERS—with **Woody Guthrie**, Willard Lampell, **Lee Hays**, and **Pete Seeger**

Pete Seeger (Almanac Houses, People's Songs, *Union Boys*, *The Weavers*, solo act, performed w/young **Mary Travers**, and oft-covered singer-songwriter/adapter: "Where Have All the Flowers Gone by the *Kingston Trio*, "One Man's Hands" by the *Highwaymen*, "Turn! Turn!" by the *Byrds*,etc.)

Lee Hays (Almanac Houses, People's Songs, *Union Boys*, *The Weavers*, oft-covered songwriter) and also with John Peter Hawes, Butch Hawes (husband of Bess Lomax—Alan's daughter), etc.and

THE UNION BOYS—Moses Asch's "house band", recording for Asch Records, with

Pete Seeger (see above and below)

Josh White (great folk performer—his presence [and that of Sonny Terry] makes at least something of an argument for the *Union Boys* as the first integrated folk group, not *The Tarriers*.

Still, the *Union Boys* were just a house recording and broadcasting group for Asch Records, and never performed in public, strengthening *The Tarriers* claim as groundbreakers in that regard)

Burl Ives (acclaimed solo performer, Oscar winning actor for *The Big Country*, Sam the Snowman on *Rudolph the Red Nosed Reindeer*, etc.)

Sonny Terry, Brownie McGhee, Tom Glazer, and sometimes

Cisco Houston, **Lee Hays**, **Woody Guthrie**, Wade Mainer, Red Rector, Fred Smith, Lily Moe Ledford, and the Coon Creek Girls.

from which emerged

THE WEAVERS—with **Pete Seeger**, **Lee Hays**, **Fred Hellerman**, **Ronnie Gilbert**, later **Erik Darling,**

Bernie Krause)

Pete Seeger (see above)

Lee Hays (see above)

Fred Hellerman (oft-covered songwriter; producer of *One More Time!* LP by *The Highwaymen*)

Ronnie Gilbert (oft-covered songwriter)

Erik Darling (the *Tarriers*, the *Rooftop Singers*)

Bernie Krause (*Weavers'* last banjo player; producer of *Homecoming* LP by *The Highwaymen*)

THE GATEWAY SINGERS—with **Lou Gottlieb** (worked for the *Kingston Trio*, sang withthe *Limeliters*) and **Travis Edmondson** (of *Bud & Travis*).

THE NEW LOST CITY RAMBLERS—with **Mike Seeger** (brother of **Pete Seeger**)

THE TARRIERS—**Erik Darling**, **Bob Carey**, **Alan Arkin**, later **Eric Weissberg,** Al Dana, Clarence Cooper, **Marshall Brickman**

Erik Darling (the *Weavers*, the *Rooftop Singers*)

Bob Carey (founding member of *The Tarriers,* later with *The Tiffany Singers*)

Alan Arkin (Tony winning and Oscar and Emmy nominated actor)

Eric Weissberg (banjoist w/Marshall Brickman, star session musician, "dueling banjos")

Marshall Brickman (*The New Journeymen*, wrote *Annie Hall* w/Woody Allen [Oscar], won Tony for *The Jersey Boys*).

THE KINGSTON TRIO—**Bob Shane**, **Dave Guard**, **Nick Reynolds**, **John Stewart**, Jim Connor,

Pat Horine, **Bill Zorn**, Roger Gambill, George Grove, **Bob Haworth**

Bob Shane (the *Kingston Trio* since its inception)

Dave Guard (the *Whisky Hill Singers*)

Nick Reynolds (the *Kingston Trio* 1957-1967, 1987-1998)

Bob Haworth (the *Kingston Trio*, the *Brothers Four*)

Bill Zorn (the *New Christy Minstrels*, *the Kingston Trio*, the *Limeliters*, the *Kingston Trio* again)

THE LIMELITERS—**Lou Gottlieb**, **Alex Hassilev**, Glenn Yarborough, Ernie Shelton,

Red Grammer, **Rick Dougherty**, **Bill Zorn**, Andy Corwin, Mack Bailey

Lou Gottlieb (the *Gateway Singers*, worked for the *Kingston Trio*, the *Limeliters*)

Alex Hassilev (the *Limeliters* since the group's inception)

Glenn Yarborough (solo career: "Baby the Rain Must Fall" and The *Folk Reunion*)

Red Grammer (singter-songwriter and children's artist)

Rick Dougherty (*The Folk Reunion*)

259

Bill Zorn (*New Christy Minstrels*, the *Kingston Trio*, the *Limeliters*, the *Kingston Trio* again)

THE HALIFAX THREE—with **Denny Doherty** (the *Mamas & the Papas*)

THE JOURNEYMEN—with Dick Weissman, **John Phillips**, **Scott McKenzie**
John Phillips (the Mamas & the Papas)
Scott McKenzie (solo artist: "San Francisco")

THE BROTHERS FOUR—**Bob Flick**, **Dick Foley**, John Paine, Mike Kirkland, Mark Pearson, Terry Lauber, **Bob Haworth**, Tom Coe
Bob Flick (with the *Brothers Four* at the group's inception and today)
Dick Foley (the *Brothers Four*, *The Folk Reunion*)
Bob Haworth (*the Kingston Trio*, the *Brothers Four*)

THE CUMBERLAND THREE—**John Stewart**, **Gil Robbins**, John Montgomery, with **Mike Settle**
John Stewart (the *Cumberland Three*, the *Kingston Trio*, songwriter: "Daydream Believer", and solo artist: "Gold")
Gil Robbins (the *Robert de Cormier Singers*, the *Belafonte Singers*, the *Cumberland Three*, sang with Oscar Brand, and the *Highwaymen*)
Mike Settle (*New Christy Minstrels*, solo artist, also played with **Jim [Roger] McGuinn**, others)

THE HIGHWAYMEN—**Bob Burnett**, **Steve Butts**, **Chan Daniels**, **Dave Fisher**, **Steve Trott**, **Gil Robbins**, Johann Helton
Bob Burnett (with the group since its inception)
Steve Butts (with the group since its inception)
Chan Daniels (an original member; died in 1975)

Dave Fisher (with the group since its inception; singer-songwriter, solo artist)

Steve Trott (an original member of the group; with the group today; a Federal Judge)

Gil Robbins (*Robert DeCormier Singers*, *Belafonte Singers*, *Cumberland Three*, with

Oscar Brand, the *Highwaymen*; choral director/arranger and actor)

THE CHAD MITCHELL TRIO—Chad Mitchell, Mike Kobluk, Joe Frazier, **John Denver**

with **Jim (Roger) McGuinn, Paul Prestopino,** etc., accompanying

John Denver (highly successful solo artist and singer-songwriter)

Jim (Roger) McGuinn (*The Byrds*)

Paul Prestopino (played backup [banjo] for *CMTrio*, *PP&M*, **Pete Seeger**, and MANY others)

THE NEW CHRISTY MINSTRELS—including **Randy Sparks, Barry McGuire, Larry Ramos,**

Mike Settle, Art Podell, Jerry Yester, Karen Black, Bill Zorn, Gaylan Taylor, etc.

Randy Sparks (successful singer-songwriter)

Barry McGuire (solo artist: "Eve of Destruction")

Larry Ramos (the *Association*)

Karen Black (Academy Award winning actress)

Mike Settle (briefly with *Cumberland Three*, roomed with **Jim [Roger] McGuinn**, solo artist)

Art Podell & **Jerry Yester** (of *the Lovin' Spoonful* with **John Sebastian**)

Bill Zorn (*New Christy Minstrels, Kingston Trio, Limeliters,* and *Kingston Trio* again)

Gaylan Taylor (the most recent *Limeliter*)

and many more, including Kenny Rogers, Kim Carnes, and future members of the *Byrds* and the *Modern Folk Quartet*

PETER , PAUL & MARY—**Peter Yarrow, Mary Travers, Noel Paul Stookey,**

with **Dick Kniss, Paul Prestopino,** etc. accompanying and **Robert DeCormier** as musical director

Peter Yarrow (songwriter: "Light One Candle")

Mary Travers (sang with **Pete Seeger** as a young girl)

Noel Paul Stookey (former comedian and MC at the Gaslight Café in Greenwich Village)

Dick Kniss (co-wrote "Sunshine on my Shoulder" with John Denver)

Paul Prestopino (played backup (banjo) for *CMTrio*, *PP&M*, **Pete Seeger,** MANY others)

Robert DeCormier (his *Robert DeCormier Singers* featured **Gil Robbins** of the *Highwaymen*)

THE ROOFTOP SINGERS—**Erik Darling**, Bill Svanoe, Lynne Taylor

Erik Darling (the *Tarriers*, the *Weavers*)

WE FIVE—with **Mike Stewart** (brother of **John Stewart**)

THE AU GO GO SINGERS—with **Stephen Stills** and **Richie Furay** (later of *Buffalo Springfield*, etc.)

THE MAMAS & THE PAPAS—**John Phillips, Denny Doherty, Michelle Phillips**, and Cass Elliott

John Phillips (the Journeymen, the Mamas & the Papas, songwriter)

Denny Doherty (the Halifax Three, the Mamas & the Papas)

Michelle Phillips (*The New Journeymen*)

THE NEW JOURNEYMEN—**John Phillips, Michelle Phillips, Marshall Brickman**
John and Michelle Phillips (*The Mamas & The Papas*)
Marshall Brickman (*The Tarriers*, Oscar-and-Tony winning writer)

and MANY more... like the Poz-Seco Singers, the Cumberland Trio, Travellers 3, Tripjacks, and Irish groups like Tommy Makem & the Clancy Brothers and The Irish Rovers, just to name a few...

followed by *THE BYRDS, BUFFALO SPRINGFIELD, CROSBY STILLS NASH & YOUNG,* and eventually back around again to folk groups, with the likes of *THE MODERN FOLK QUARTET* and *SCHOONER FARE...*etc.

This does not even begin to address the variety of songs by outstanding solo folk artists covered by these groups or the various contacts and connections made by these groups with other folk performers. Among those whose songs were covered by these folk groups and/or those who shared the stage with them were (are): Pete Seeger, Bob Dylan, Phil Ochs, Ed McCurdy, Oscar Brand, Lee Hays, Fred Hellerman, Noel Paul Stookey, Carolyn Hester, Joan Baez, Buffy St. Marie, Dave Van Ronk, John Denver, Ian Tyson, and so many, many more.

The folk music scene, despite its parallel roots on either coast, kept and has kept to a pretty tight, interconnected community from the earliest stages of the folk revival right through into the present. The current folk community, although much more diverse than earlier generations, remains connected and supported today in no small part due to the efforts of the World Folk Music Association: hence our next Appendix. Read on!

APPENDIX D

WFMA Honors

Over the years, the World Folk Music Association has honored a number of individuals and even groups for their contributions and endeavors.

THE KATE WOLF MEMORIAL AWARD

Established on Valentine's Day, 1987, in memory of Kate Wolf, it is now awarded annually to the performer who best epitomizes the music and spirit of the late California singer-songwriter. The singer or singer-songwriter chosen for this award receives a grant, a plaque, and an invitation to perform at the annual benefit concert. Selection of the honoree is made by a committee consisting of Kate's fellow performers and friends. The Award is presented at the Annual WFMA Benefit Concert in January of the following year.

1988	Utah Phillips
1989	Christine Lavin
1990	Rosalie Sorrels
1991	Robin Batteau
1992	Wavy Gravy (Hugh Romney)
1993	Peter Yarrow
1994	Crow Johnson
1995	Nanci Griffith

1996   Jack Hardy

1997   Tom Chapin

1998   David Buskin

1999   Nina Gerber

2000   Noel Paul Stookey

2001   The Kennedys

2002   Anne Hills

2003   David Masengill

2004   Tom Rowe (presented posthumously, in January of 2005)

2005   The Shaw Brothers

THE WFMA LIFETIME ACHIEVEMENT AWARD

Established in 1993-1994, the Lifetime Achievement Award is presented annually to someone who has made sustained contributions to folk music over a period of many years. The year is when the award was presented.

1994   Odetta

1995   Lou Gottlieb

1996   Oscar Brand

1997   Bob Gibson

1998   John Denver (presented posthumously)

1999   Tommy Makem

2000   Rod Kennedy

2001   John Stewart

2002   Joe Glazer

2003   Carolyn Hester

2004 Dave Van Ronk (presented posthumously)

2005 Dick Cerri

2006 Tom Paxton

THE JOHN DENVER AWARD

The John Denver Award was established in 1999 to acknowledge his music and the many contributions he has made to make our planet a better place. The year is when the award was presented. It has not been awarded every year.

1999 Milt Okun

2000 Kenn Roberts

2001 Bill Danoff

2003 Tom Wisner

2004 Greg Artzner and Terry Leonino (Magpie)

2006 Dawn Publications

With its awards, the WFMA has recognized veterans of The Folk Revival and "The Great Folk Music Scare" as well as newer folk artists, and through their endeavors the WFMA has kept the ever-evolving folk music tradition alive. Dick Cerri deserves much of the credit for the success of the World Folk Music Association, and the WFMA continues to support folk performers, advocating for them and celebrating their diverse talents. From the broadside ballads of the 16th century through the efforts of scholars like Francis James Child, Cecil Sharp, John Lomax, Alan Lomax, Ruth Crawford and Charles Seeger,. folk music has come a long way. Today, the creative scholarship of Oscar Brand continues their work, along with historians like Jeff Place and Guy Logsdon, while a new generations of folk artists follows in the footsteps of groups like the Weavers, the Kingston Trio, the Brothers Four, the Limeliters, the Highwaymen, and Peter, Paul, & Mary. The WFMA is a place where both the older and newer strands of the folk music scene can and do share a stage and a commitment to keep folk music a vibrant and vital force in American culture.

SOURCES

BOOKS

The Billboard Book of Number One Hits by Fred Bronson, New York: Billboard
Publications, Inc. (1985)

The Billboard Book of American Singing Groups by Jay Warner, New York: Billboard
Publications, Inc. (1992)

Folk Music by Peter Sieling, Broomall, Pennsylvania: Mason Crest Publishers, Inc. (2003)
from the *North American Folklore* Series, Dr. Alan Jabbour series consultant

Folk Songs by Peter Sieling, Broomall, Pennsylvania: Mason Crest Publishers, Inc. (2003)
from the *North American Folklore* Series, Dr. Alan Jabbour series consultant

The Music of the American Folk Song by Ruth Crawford Seeger, etc. Rochester, NY: U. of
Rochester Press (2001)

Sixties People by Jane and Michael Stern, New York: Alfred A. Knopf (1990)

The Top Ten by Bob Gilbert and Gary Theroux, New York: Fireside/Simon & Schuster
(1982)

Chronicles—Volume One by Bob Dylan, New York: Simon & Schuster (2004)
Rise Up Singing, Edited by Peter Blood & Annie Patterson, Bethlehem, Pennsylvania: A
Sing Out! Publication (1992)

The Mayor of MacDougall Street by Dave Van Ronk, etc., Cambridge, MA: Da Capo (2006)

Which Side Are You On? An Inside History of the Folk Music Revival in America by Dick Weissman, Continuum International Publishing Group (2006)

MAGAZINES, PERIODICALS, etc.

"Tin Pan Alley—Reality in Academia", *Time*, October 6, 1961, pp. 49-50

"Singles Sales Lag—New Artists Should Stay Single 'Til They're Ready", *TV Radio Mirror*, Atlantic Edition, Vol. 57, No. 1, December 1961, p. 80H

"Top 50 Records of the Month—Best Selling New LPs" *TV Radio Mirror*, Midwest Edition, Vol. 57, No. 2, January 1962, p. 76F

"Around the World With The Highwaymen", *Rock and Roll Songs*, a Charlton Publication, Vol. 7, No. 27, January 1962, p. 14

"Spotlight on the Highwaymen", *National Musician,* the official journal of the American Federation of Musicians of the United States and Canada, Vol. LXI, No. 1, July 1962, p. 39

"Instant Success", ESQUIRE: *Back to College Issue*, September 1962

"A Bumper Crop of Hot Singles", *Cash Box*, Vol. XXIII, Number 4, October 7 1961, cover story

"The Next Hit by the Highwaymen—NME Poll Winners Supplement", *New Musical Express*, No. 777, December 1 1961, cover story

Sources

"Hullabaloo, guest starring The Highwaymen", *TV Roundup for Western Illinois: Chicago's Sunday American*, April 11-17 1965, p. 11

Billboard Music Week, July 7, 1962

"Black Notes for the Highwaymen", *Seventeen*, December 1963, pp. 94-95

"Right to Sing: The Ballad of Washington Square, Spring 1961" by Jay Maeder, *Big Town Song Book, Daily News Big Town*, June 17, 2004

Jim Lundstrom, "Highwaymen dust off acoustic guitars for reunion concert at PAC" *Appleton Post-Crescent*, Appleton, Wisconsin, 2005

PUBLISHED MUSIC, etc.

"Michael", United Artists Music, traditional: new words and arrangement by David FisherNew York: Keys-Hansen, Inc. (1961)

"Cotton Fields", Westside Music, by Huddie Ledbetter/new words and arrangement by David Fisher, New York: Hansen (1962)

"The Gypsy Rover (The Whistling Gypsy)" words and music by Leo Maguire, Box & Cox Publications, New York: Keys-Hansen (1962)

Highwaymen Folk Song Album, The Highwaymen, New York: Hansen Publications (1962)

Hootenanny Sing! New York: Hollis Music, Inc. (1963)

271

LINER NOTES/ALBUMS/RECORDED SOURCES , etc.
LPs--

The Highwaymen, UAL 3125/UAS 6125, New York: United Artists (1960)

Standing Room Only! UAL 3168/UAS 6168, New York: United Artists (1961)

Encore, UAL 3225/UAS 6225, produced by Don Costa Productions Inc./GLG Productions, cover photograph by Frank Guana, New York: United Artists (1962)

March On, Brothers, UAL 3245/UAS 6245, produced by Milt Okun, New York: United Artists (1962)

Hootenanny With The Highwaymen, UAL 3294/UAS 6294/UALS 8049, liner notes by Ed McCurdy, New York: United Artists (1963)

One More Time! UAL 3323/UAS 6323, a "GLG" Production, cover design by Norman Art Studio, NY: UA (1964)

Homecoming! UAL 3348, recorded live at Wesleyan University, a GLG Production/ assisted by Bernie Krause/ Recording Engineer: Tory Brainard, New York: United Artists (1964)

The Spirit & The Flesh UAL 3397, produced by GLG Productions, liner notes written by David Fisher, New York: United Artists (1964)

On A New Road ABC-522/ABCS-522, produced by Bob Crewe for GLG Productions, Musical Director David Fisher, Arranged and Conducted by Charles Calello, liner notes by Rick Ward, cover design and photos: ARW Productions Inc., New York: ABC-Paramount (1965)

Stop! Look! & Listen! ABC-543/ABCS-543, a GLG Production, produced and arranged by David Fisher, Production Supervisor: Ken Greengrass, Sound Engineer: Phil Ramone, cover design: ARW Productions Inc., liner design by: Joe Lebow, ABC-Paramount (1966)

The World of Folk Music, starring Oscar Brand, episode with guests The Highwaymen courtesy of United Artists, Social Security Administration—U.S. Department of Health-Education-and-Welfare (1963)

The World of Folk Music, starring Oscar Brand, episode with guests The Highwaymen courtesy of ABC-Paramount, Social Security Administration—U.S. Department of Health-Education-and-Welfare (1965)

45s--

Michael/Santiano, UA 258/UA 67 007, United Artists release 9-21-1960

Michael/Santiano/Sinner Man/ Irish Work Song, UA 68 104, United Artists international release 1961

Michael/Cotton Fields/Gypsy Rover/Whisky in the Jar, UAX 1506, United Artists international release 1962

Los Bandoleros "The Highwaymen" with Michael/Santiano/Carnavalito/O Pecador (Sinner Man), HU 067-45)
Hispavox—Spain, United Artists international release 1961

The Bird Man/Cindy O Cindy, UA 475, from "L'Uomo di Alcatraz", United Artists release {nat'l/int'l] 6-25-1962

Well, Well, Well/I Know Where I'm Going, UA 540, United Artists release 10-10-1962

I'll Fly Away/Universal Soldier, UA 647, United Artists release, September 1963.

The Sinking of the Reuben James/Bon Soir, UA 695, United Artists release, January 1964.

Michael/Cotton Fields, HIT 7018/2 455-237-UA, Japan: Golden Coupling and Mascot Series

Michael '65/Puttin' On The Style, UA 801, United Artists release 11-12-1964

I'll Show You the Way/Never a Thought for Tomorrow, ABC 10716, ABC Paramount release, 08-19-1965.

She's Not There/Little Bird, Little Bird, ABC 10801, ABC-Paramount release 03-31-1966

CDs--

Michael Row the Boat Ashore: the best of the Highwaymen, EMI 0777-7-963342-2 5, produced by Don Costa, Dave Fisher, Milt Okun, GLG productions, Bernie Krause, Chan Daniels; compilation produced and compiled by Ron Furmanek, Steve Kolanjian, Paul Surrat, Dave Fisher; liner notes by Dave Fisher and Steve Kolanjian; track annotations and discography by Steve Kolanjian; digitally remastered by Ron Furmanek at Capitol Recording Studios, Hollywood, CA, June 1991. Copyright 1992.

Back 2 Back Hits—The Kingston Trio & The Highwaymen, EMI-Capitol Music 72438-19463-2 9. Copyright 1997.

Still Rowing—The Highwaymen, newly recorded and mastered in Los Angeles, CA; David Fisher/Dayfish Music, ca. 1999.

Sources

Two Classic Albums from The Highwaymen—The Highwaymen/Standing Room Only, EMI
& Collector's Choice Music. Copyright 2000.

The Highwaymen: Live at Rye, New York, courtesy of Steve Butts, July 2000.

Johann Helton—Where Mountains End and Clouds Begin, produced by Johann and Susan
Clay Helton, Goddess Sound Productions, published by Mystrionic Music (ASCAP).
Copyright 2000.

In Concert, recorded live in New York, Connecticut, and Idaho; compiled by Steve Butts;
mastered by Don Cunningham and Johann Helton at Cunningham Audio in Boise, Idaho.
Copyright 2002.

Love's Way—Dave Fisher, Dayfish Music, arranged and produced by Dave Fisher and
Rocky Davis, liner notes by A.B. Clyde. Copyright 2002.

The Water of Life—a Celtic collection, recorded at JoTown Records in Boise, Idaho;
engineered by Johann Helton; mastered by Dave Fisher and Don Cunningham at
Cunningham Audio in Boise, Idaho; cover photo by Stephen J. Butts. Copyright 2004.

When the Village Was Green – Recorded Live at the Blackstone River Theater, mastered at
Cunningham Audio in Boise, Idaho; mixed by Dave Fisher; liner notes by Nick Noble;
photos by Joe Deuel and Mark Swirsky. Copyright 2007.

The Highwaymen—The Folk Hits Collection, Varese Vintage Records/Varese Sarabande.
Copyright 2007.
Modern Folk Song Collection, Japan.

"Professor of Folk Music, with Stephen J. Butts", *University of the Air*, Wisconsin Public Radio, 2002.

Cassettes--

11ᵗʰ Annual World Folk Music Association Benefit Concert, 1996 Lisner Concert. Copyright 1997, WFMA.

Moses Henry MacNaughten, privately made cassettes of original music and interview responses, 2003.

VHS--

This Land is Your Land: the Folk Years, RHINO Home Video; filmed May 21 & 22, 2002 at Carnegie Mellon University: WQED Pittsburgh.

POSTERS/ADS, etc.

"3 Blockbusters" promo, *Cashbox*, January 20, 1962

"The Highwaymen" poster for Concert at Westchester County Center, White Plains, NY; April 28ᵗʰ, 1963.

"The Highwaymen" poster for Concert at American University, February 28ᵗʰ, 1964.

"Watch Out! The Highwaymen are Back!" ad, *Billboard Music on Campus*, March 27, 1965, p. 51.

"A Night of Stars—The Highwaymen, Thursday, May 6, 1965", *Official Program: Dedication Week of the Bayfront Center*, St. Petersburg, Florida. May 106, 1965.

Sources

ONLINE SOURCES

"The Highwaymen—Biography" by Bruce Eder, *allmusic*, allmusic.com.

"The 1996 Benefit Lisner Concert" and "The Original Highwaymen", *World Folk Music Association*, January 1996, wfma.net.

"Top of the Newsletter III – Return of the Blarney: Folklore", *BookAgain*, bookagain.com/folklore.

"Jurist Trott in Residence at U." *University of Utah S.J. Quinney College of Law*—News & Events, 04-05-2002, www.law.utah.edu.

"Stephen Butts", *International Directory of Musicians*, www.musicbase.org.

"Gaslight Café and Kettle of Fish", *Walkin' New York*, www.newpony.com.

"Liner notes for Tom Paxton's *Ramblin' Boy*", *Richie Unterberger*, richieunterberger.com.

"Folk Music-- Definition" *Folk Music* by Maryl Neff, www.coe.ufl.edu

"Cecil Sharp—Biography" *Cecil Sharp* by David Sutcliffe, http:homepage.ntlworld.com

"Alan Lomax" Alan Lomax, www.alanlomax.com

"Huddie Ledbetter, aka Leadbelly" *Leadbelly*, http:/leadbelly.lanl.gov

"The Contemplator's Short History of Broadside Ballads", *Folk Music of England, Scotland, Ireland, Wales, and America*, http://www.contemplator.com/folk.html

"Top Hits of 1961" *Spunout Central*, spunoutcentral.com/1961

"Top Hits of 1962" *Spunout Central*, spunoutcentral.com/1962

"The Top Requested Songs—Hits of 1961", *Pop Culture Madness*, popculturemadness.com

"The Top Requested Songs—Hits of 1962", *Pop Culture Madness*, popculturemadness.com

"YE Singles (Pop) 1961" *Cash Box*,
members.aol.com/_ht_a/randypny/cashbox/1961YESP.html

"YE Singles (Pop) 1962" *Cash Box*,
members.aol.com/_ht_a/randypny/cashbox/1962YESP.html

"The Ed Sullivan Show", "Hootenanny", and "Hullabaloo", *TV Tome*, tvtome.com

"Triumvirat..." *Triumvirat*, www.geocities.co.jp/HeartLand-Icho/
1130/remasters/remasters.html

"Participant Biographies—The Hon. Stephen S. Trott", *The Cooperating Witness
Conundrum: Is Justice Obtainable?* Jacob Burns Ethic Center, Cardozo,
www.cardozo.yu.edu

"Wesleyan University: A Brief History", *About Wesleyan*, www.wesleyan.edu

"Biography", *The Tim Robbins Page*, www.timrobbins.com

"John Stewart" by Bruce Eder, *allmusic*, allmusic.com

"David Robbins", *David Robbins* Music, DavidRobbinsMusic.com

Sources

"Dave Fisher (IV)", "A.B. Clyde", "Rocky Davis", "Renny Temple", "Mose Henry", etc. *Internet Movie Data Base*, imdb.com

"The Highwaymen", *TVC*, cheerful.com

"Trott, Stephen S.", *Judges of the United States Courts*, air.fjc.gov

"Stephen J. Butts—Lawrence University", *HEDS*, heds.fandm.edu

"Gil Robbins", E. *Henry David Music Publishers*, ehenrydavid.com

"How I Narrowly Escaped Insanity" by Alex Kozinski, *Law In Popular Culture Collections*, from *UCLA Law Review*, Vol. 48, Number 6, August 2001, E-texts, tarlton.law.utexas.edu

"Oscar Brand", *University of Manitoba: Archives and Special Collections*, www.umanitoba.ca

"Oscar Brand Biography", *Oscar Brand*, oscarbrand.com

World Folk Music Association, wfma.net

The Original Highwaymen., originalhighwaymen.com (official group website)

The Fabulous Limeliters, limeliters.com

And various other online folk encyclopedias, web pages, etc.

OTHER PRIMARY SOURCES/DOCUMENTS, etc.

Letter from David H. Trott to Mr. Robert E. Short, Procter and Gamble, 10/19/1959, courtesy of Steve Trott.

Letter from Lewis H. Titterton, Vice President in charge of Radio and Television Programming, Compton Advertising Inc. to Mr. David H. Trott, 10/27/1959, courtesy of Steve Trott.

Notes taken by Steve Trott, November, 1959, courtesy of Steve Trott.

Letter from David H. Trott to Lewis H. Titterton, 12/31/1959, courtesy of Steve Trott.

Letter from Lewis H. Titterton to David H. Trott, 1/12/1960, courtesy of Steve Trott.

Letter from Ken Greengrass to Dave Fisher, 1/27/1960, courtesy of Steve Trott.

"CHUM Hit Parade", *CHUM Chart*, CHUM 1050, Toronto, Canada, for week of July 17, 1961.

"Billboard Hot 100", *Billboard Music Week*, week of July 24, 1961.

"CHUM Hit Parade", *CHUM Chart*, CHUM 1050, Toronto, Canada, for week of October 9, 1961.

"CHUM Hit Parade", *CHUM Chart*, CHUM 1050, Toronto, Canada, for week of December 4, 1961.

"CHUM Hit Parade", *CHUM Chart*, CHUM 1050, Toronto, Canada, for week of January 8, 1962.

Sources

"KFWB Fabulous Forty Survey", *KFWB Number 1 in Los Angeles*, KFWB 98, for week ending March 9, 1962.

"The Highwaymen", *Blackstone River Theater Schedule of Events*, September-December 2004. p. 1.

"Let's Get Together", *World Folk Music Association 20th Anniversary Weekend* program, 1/14-15/05, . J. Votel, Ed.

INTERVIEWS/CORRESPONDENCE, etc.

Letters/Email and other correspondence, taped interviews, personal conversations, etc. with Steve Butts, Bob Burnett, Dave Fisher, Steve Trott, Oscar Brand, Ken Greengrass, Moses Henry MacNaughten, Elaine Haagen, Cathy Burnett, Carol Trott, Johann Helton, Tim Noble, Maggie Noble, Jared Wickware, etc.

MISCELLANEOUS

"The Highwaymen", *EMI Legends of Rock n' Roll*, collector's card #24, from EMI release #96334. Copyright 1991.

Liner notes from *Hootenanny Florida Union* LP, 1963

Liner notes by Mary A. Meehan from *Folk Song and Minstrelsy* and American *Folk Singers and Balladeers*, from The Classics Record Library, Vanguard Recordings. Copyrights 1964.

Liner notes by Jeff Place and John Herzog from *Do-Re-Mi: Songs of Rags and Riches*, from Smithsonian Folkways , 2007.

Liner notes by Guy Logsdon and Jeff Place from That's *Why We're Marching: World War II and the American Folk Movement*, from Smithsonian Folkways, 2007.

5K Race Results, coolrunning.com

ABOUT THE AUTHOR

A native New Yorker, Richard E. "Nick" Noble has spent most of his adult life in New England. After earning his M.A. in History from Trinity College in Connecticut, Nick joined the teaching ranks, a vocation he has followed for more than a quarter century now. Currently, he is on the history faculty of the Advanced Math & Science Academy Charter School in Marlboro, Massachusetts. Nick enjoys writing about history, while he acknowledges that, like many historians, he is not "too much encumbered by facts". He also enjoys listening to and singing along with folk music, much to the chagrin of his teenage son and his very patient wife. He has written several books—including *The Touch of Time, Brantwood, Fences of Stone*, and *To Honor the Trust*—and has contributed to a number of others. This newest book is a real labor of love. Folk music has played a huge role in his life, and Nick has used folk songs from time to time in his classes. Nick is also the current host of "The Folk Revival" on WICN in Worcester, where he now resides. This, then, is an opportunity for him to give just a little bit back, using the story of the original Highwaymen as a canvas on which to paint a history of folk music. Of course he's preaching to the choir. Still, while perusing its pages the reader might just start to hum along.

INDEX

"NUMBER #1" NOTES

This is a fairly comprehensive index, but a few of notes are in order.

- The original Highwaymen are **not** indexed as a group, because they are mentioned throughout the book. Members of the group **are** specifically indexed as individuals.

- Single songs are **only** indexed in a **limited** way. Just five songs are thoroughly indexed: "Michael" and "Cotton Fields" because of their Billboard success, "The Gypsy Rover" because it was also (along with the aforementioned) released as sheet music, "Santiano" because it was the group's first A-side **and** because of its phenomenal success in France, and "Number #1" because it contributed the title of this book.

- All Highwaymen albums (LPs **and** CDs) are indexed, along with any other full-length releases mentioned within these pages.

- The list of sources is indexed only in relation to the main text, so some less significant details may have been omitted when indexing those pages.

- The Appendices were completed before the rest of the book, so they may be missing some more recent information. For example, the newest World Folk Music Association award information may also be missing.

- The newest Highwaymen CD—the never-before-released MIT concert from October of 1963—now has a name. *The Cambridge Tapes*, issued in late February of 2009 on the FolkEra label features a two-disc collection of a long "lost" Highwaymen performance.

- Long-time Highwaymen friend and supporter John Keeler deserves mention for his intrepid initiative in taping that MIT concert back in 1963, preserving a piece of folk music history and making possible this newest Highwaymen CD.

- Any remaining errors (and I'm sure there are plenty) are entirely my responsibility. Mea culpa. And don't forget to check out the website at www.originalhighwaymen.com

- Finally, an update on two of the original Highwaymen. At this writing, David Fisher is at home in Rye, NY, recovering from a recent bout with heart disease, while Bob Burnett is back home from the hospital after undergoing a second surgery to treat brain cancer. Both are doing well, and the original Highwaymen intend to keep on making music for some time to come.

There is no limit to folk music. As Louis Armstrong once said: "*All music is folk music. I ain't never heard a horse sing a song.*" There is also no limit to the patience of all those folks who have been waiting for the arrival of this book. Thanks again to everyone at Outskirts Press. Michelle—you are wonderful!

Also thanks for all their love and support to my friends and colleagues at WICN – Worcester Public Radio – "New England's Jazz and Folk Station" at 90.5 FM or online at wicn.org. Listen to THE FOLK REVIVAL every Thursday from 7-11 PM Eastern Standard Time. You might just hear more than a few of the songs you've been reading about (if you actually made it this far).

A heartfelt thank you to my AMSA colleagues for providing a wonderful atmosphere in which to work as educators, and for putting up with their fellow teacher's "other life" as a hard-core folkie.

And very special thanks to my loving family, without whom I am nothing, and with whom everything is possible.

Nick Noble
March, 2009

Printed in the United States
220626BV00003B/1/P

9 781432 738099